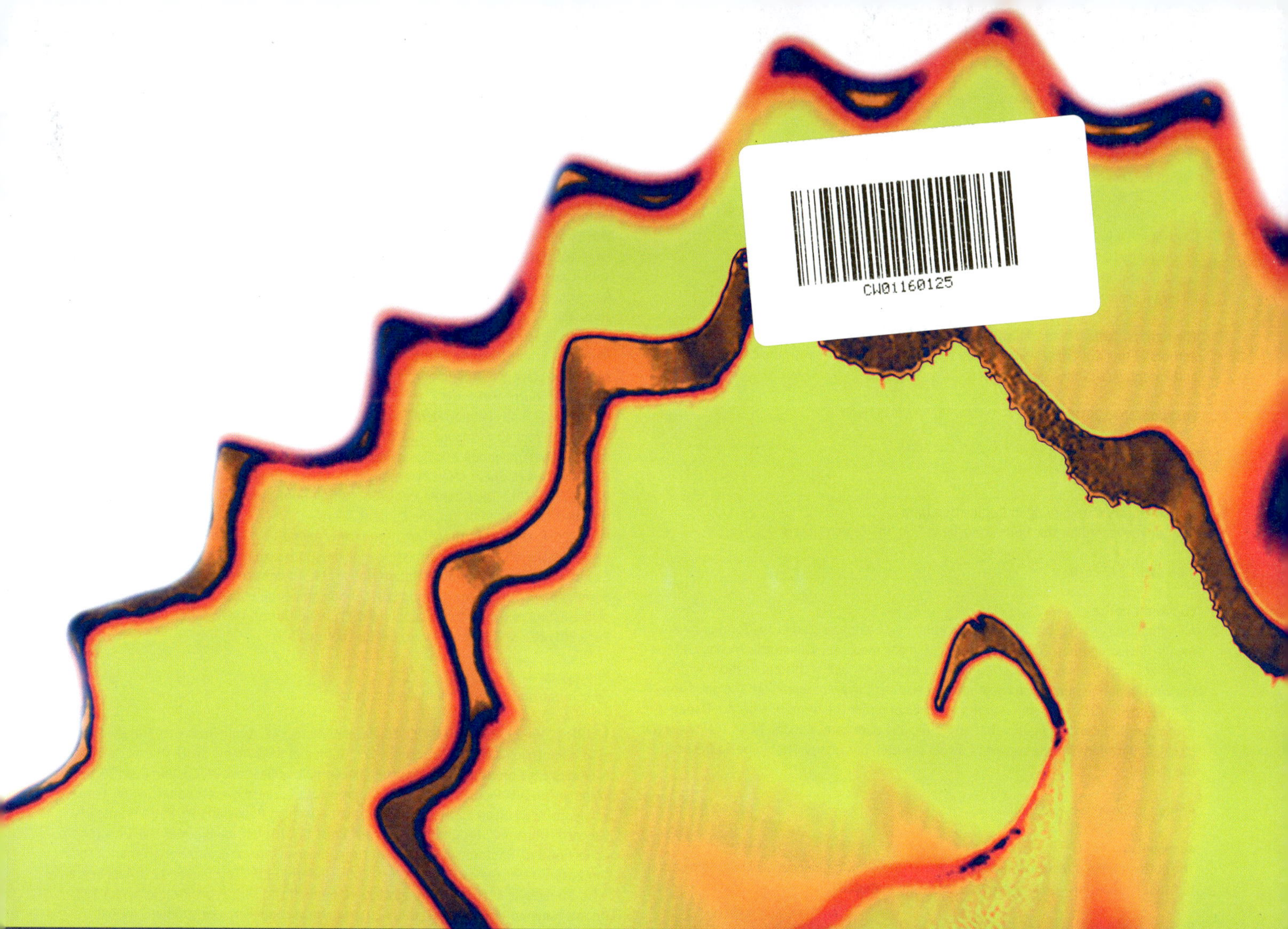

Edexcel GCSE (9-1)
English Language Reading and Writing

Securing key skills with exam preparation

Reading sections by Esther Menon and David Grant
Writing sections by Martin Phillips and Emma Clark

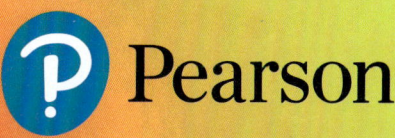

Published by Pearson Education Limited, 80 Strand, London, WC2R 0RL.

www.pearsonschoolsandfecolleges.co.uk

Design and cover illustration by Poppy Marks, Pearson Education Ltd
Text and illustrations © Pearson Education Ltd 2018
Typeset and illustrated by Kamae Design
Illustrated by Jo and Terry at KJA Artists Illustration Agency and Sam Bridge
Produced by Haremi Ltd
Cover illustration © Alamy Stock Photo/PhotosIndia.com LLC
Picture research by Aptara

The right of Esther Menon, Martin Phillips, Emma Clark and David Grant, to be identified as authors of this work has been asserted by them in accordance with the Copyright, Designs and Patents Act 1988.

First published 2018

21 20 19 18
10 9 8 7 6 5 4 3 2 1

British Library Cataloguing in Publication Data
A catalogue record for this book is available from the British Library

ISBN 978 1 292 24703 8

Copyright notice
All rights reserved. No part of this publication may be reproduced in any form or by any means (including photocopying or storing it in any medium by electronic means and whether or not transiently or incidentally to some other use of this publication) without the written permission of the copyright owner, except in accordance with the provisions of the Copyright, Designs and Patents Act 1988 or under the terms of a licence issued by the Copyright Licensing Agency, Barnard's Inn, 86 Fetter Lane, London EC4A 1EN (www.cla.co.uk). Applications for the copyright owner's written permission should be addressed to the publisher.

Printed in Slovakia by Neografia

Acknowledgements
The authors and publisher would like to thank the following individuals and organisations for their kind permission to reproduce copyright material.

Page 018, 024, 025, 026, 027, 028, 029, 033: *The Times* / News Licensing.
Page 034: Real Estate Management (UK) Limited.
Page 035, 036, 041: Copyright Guardian News & Media Ltd 2018.
Page 048, 049: © Telegraph Media Group Limited 2014.
Page 051: From *The Soul of a Butterfly: Reflections on Life's Journey* by Muhammad Ali with Hana Yasmeen. Copyright © 2004 by Muhammad Ali Family Trust dated October 22, 2002, and Hana Yasmeen Ali. Reprinted with the permission of Simon & Schuster, Inc. All rights reserved.; "Muhammad Ali™; Rights of publicity and Persona Rights: Muhammad Ali Enterprise LLC.ali.com".
Page 052: The Economist Newspaper Limited, Obituary: Muhammad Ali, June 11, 2016.
Page 054, 055, 060, 061: Chris Stewart, Sort Of Books, *A Parrot in the Pepper Tree: A Sequel to Driving Over Lemons*, 2009.
Page 056, 059, 062, 065: Except from *In The Shadow Of Man* by Jane Goodall. Copyright © by Hugo and Jane van Lawick Goodall. Reprinted by permission of Houghton Mifflin Harcourt publishing company. All rights reserved.; Jane Goodall, Orion books, *In the Shadow of Man*, 2010.

Page 056, 058, 059, 062: Copyright Guardian News & Media Ltd 2018.
Page 078: PRESS ASSOCIATION.
Page 080: BBC copyright material reproduced courtesy of the British Broadcasting Corporation. All rights reserved.
Page 090: Courtesy of Nelson Mandela foundation.
Page 091: For quotes reproduced from the speeches of Winston S. Churchill: Reproduced with permission of Curtis Brown, London on behalf of The Estate of Winston S. Churchill. © The Estate of Winston S. Churchill.
Page 105: Excerpted from *The Tobacconist* by Robert Seethaler, copyright © 2012 by Kein & Aber AG Zurich-Berlin, English translation copyright © 2016 by Charlotte Collins. Reproduced with permission from House of Anansi Press Inc., Toronto. www.houseofanansi.com.; *The Tobacconist* by Robert Seethaler, Reproduced with permission of the Licensor through PLSclear.
Page 116: Stuart Maconie, Reach Publishing Services Limited, 'Britain's worst kept guilty secret: We can't get enough of fast food', October 22, 2011.
Page 120: Courtesy of Crisis.
Page 156, 177: Alix Palmer, Fleet Street Memories, Aberfan Disaster, October 7, 2016.
Page 159: From *An Astronaut's Guide to Life on Earth: What Going to Space Taught Me about Ingenuity, Determination, and Being Prepared for Anything* by Chris Hadfield. Copyright © 2013 by Chris Hadfield. Used by permission of Little, Brown and Company.; Excerpted.
Page 172: © 2017 The Atlantic Media Co., as first published in TheAtlantic.com All rights reserved. Distributed by Tribune Content Agency.
Page 200: Excerpt(s) from *My Family and Other Animals* by Gerald Durrell, copyright © 1956 by Gerald Durrell. Used by permission of Viking Books, an imprint of Penguin Publishing Group, a division of Penguin Random House LLC. All rights reserved.; Reproduced with permission of Curtis Brown Group Ltd, London on behalf of Lee Durrell as the Beneficiary of The Estate of Gerald Durrell Copyright © Gerald Durrell 1956.
Page 201, 202: © Telegraph Media Group Limited 2015.

Photographs
(Key: b-bottom; c-centre; l-left; r-right; t-top)

123RF: 123RF 21, 25, 61t, 71, 78, 176, Pavel Klimenko 48, Armin Rose 61b, Travelwitness 104t, Khuntnop Asawachiwantorngul 127, Goldenkb 144l; **Alamy Stock Photo:** Mark Draisey 6, LifeStyle 8, Chronicle 10, Lordprice Collection 23, Stills Press 27, Cristian Gusa 35, Jim Wileman 39, DPA Picture Alliance 52, Abramorama/Coutesy Everett Collection 56, Perry van Munster 85, Ryan Rodrick Beiler 89, Clynt Garnham Publishing 95, Peter Horree 98, Lancashire Images/Stockimo 99r, Pictorial Press Ltd 101, Jeffrey Blackler 106, Directphoto Collection 110, PhotoAlto 112, Hemis 118tl, Universal Images Group North America LLC/DeAgostini 118tr, Simon Rawles 118b, Colin Underhill 119l, Faiz Balabil 121l, Alex Segre 121c, Paul Doyle 121r, UrbanImages 165, NASA Archive 178, ICP-UK/incamerastock 188, Dennis Hallinan 199l; **DACS:** © DACS 2018 98; **Newscom:** Piero Oliosi/Polaris 68, 69l; **PA Images:** PA/PA Archive 155; **Shutterstock:** Dark Moon Pictures 15, Slava Gerj 16, Sam-Whitfield1 17, Ingus Kruklitis 37, Naeblys 47, Sipa Press/REX 49, Kristof Degreef 65, NRT 69r, Steve Meddle/ITV 79, Yobidaba 90, Granger/REX 94, Robert Kneschke 96, Jaromir Chalabala 99l, Evannovostro 100, Ppictures 104b, Foxy Burrow 109, Damian Ryszawy 119r, Greg Epperson 144r, Chris Fourie 181, Mila Supinskaya Glashchenko 190, Sasa Prudkov 199r.

All other images © Pearson Education

Notes from the publisher
Pearson has robust editorial processes, including answer and fact checks, to ensure the accuracy of the content in this publication, and every effort is made to ensure this publication is free of errors. We are, however, only human, and occasionally errors do occur. Pearson is not liable for any misunderstandings that arise as a result of errors in this publication, but it is our priority to ensure that the content is accurate. If you spot an error, please do contact us at resourcescorrections@pearson.com so we can make sure it is corrected.

Contents

How to use this book — iv

1 Understanding and interpreting meaning — 6

2 The writer at work: language — 14

3 The writer at work: structure — 34

4 Focusing on language and structure — 50

5 Synthesising and comparing — 54

6 Evaluation — 68

7 Word and sentence choices — 84

8 Creative and imaginative writing — 98

9 Transactional writing — 110

Preparing for your exams: Paper 1 — 124

Preparing for your exams: Paper 2 — 152

Assessment test — 196

English terms — 206

How to use this book

The purpose of this book is to help you develop the knowledge and skills covered in the Edexcel English Language GCSE course, and to fully understand how you will be assessed in the exam.

Every year, Edexcel examiners write a report outlining the things that students across the country did well in the exam, and what they could have done better. The key information from those reports, along with other essential advice, is presented in the **Examiner Tip boxes** that you will find throughout this book.

Units 1–9: Skills for English Language GCSE

These units in the book cover the key subject skills that you need to develop in order to do well in the exam. At the beginning of each unit you will be shown which **Assessment Objectives (AOs)** the content relates to, as well as which **Exam Questions** test the skill. A series of **Activities** will help you develop your skills, before a final **Mini-assessment** and **Self-assessment checklist** at the end of each unit give you the chance to test your skills using tasks similar to those you will encounter in the exam.

Units 1–9: text extracts

The activities in Units 1–9 are based on a wide range of fiction and non-fiction text extracts, like those you will analyse or create in the exam. The text extracts for these units are included in the book. They are also available for teachers to access in the **free online resources**. It is strongly recommended that teachers download and print these extracts so that students can practise the key exam skill of annotating their extracts. Throughout the book, printable resources are indicated by this icon.

Preparing for your exams

Preparing for your exams includes step-by-step guidance on every exam question type that you will face in Paper 1 and Paper 2. For each exam question, content includes:

- **What is the examiner looking for?** – what is being tested.
- **Question format** – how the question will be worded and the marks available.
- **Timing** – suggested timings for each question.
- **Key steps diagram** – simple step-by-step guidance on tackling the question.
- **Activities** – structured tasks that walk you through the key steps.
- **Final task** – skills practice using a final exam-style question.

Assessment test: this final unit includes a full **Sample Paper 1 and Paper 2**. Teachers will find a linked mark scheme in the free online resources accompanying this book.

Preparing for your exams: text extracts

The text extracts needed to complete the activities in Preparing for your exams are not included in the book. They must be downloaded and printed by teachers in order for students to annotate them and then use them to complete the activities. Throughout the book, printable resources are indicated by this icon.

How to use this book

Teachers must access the free online resources

The free online resources accompanying this book include downloadable versions of the text extracts used throughout, as well as a mark scheme linked to the sample exam papers in the final unit. It is essential that teachers use these free online resources so that students can practise annotating extracts and complete the tasks set in Preparing for your exams. Follow these steps to access the resources:

1. Go to http://www.pearsonschools.co.uk/freeenglish and place an order for Pearson Edexcel GCSE English FREE Resources.
2. You should receive an email from our Subscription site asking you to accept the Purchase Terms and Conditions.
3. If you are an existing ActiveLearn user, the free resources will now appear in your library when you log in to ActiveLearn.

If you are not an existing ActiveLearn user, you will be sent a code that will enable you to Register on ActiveLearn.

1. To Register on ActiveLearn, go to www.pearsonactivelearn.com
2. Click on Register and follow the on-screen instructions.
3. Once you have registered for the free resources, login with your username and password and the title will appear in your Library.

You can now download the free resources to a location of your choice.

Edexcel GCSE English Language Assessment Objectives

Students must:

READING	
AO1	• Identify and interpret explicit and implicit information and ideas. • Select and synthesise evidence from different texts
AO2	Explain, comment on and analyse how writers use language and structure to achieve effects and influence readers, using relevant subject terminology to support their views
AO3	Compare writers' ideas and perspectives, as well as how these are conveyed, across two or more texts
AO4	Evaluate texts critically and support this with appropriate textual references
WRITING	
AO5	• Communicate clearly, effectively and imaginatively, selecting and adapting tone, style and register for different forms, purposes and audiences • Organise information and ideas, using structural and grammatical features to support coherence and cohesion of texts
AO6	Use a range of vocabulary and sentence structures for clarity, purpose and effect, with accurate spelling and punctuation

1 Understanding and interpreting meaning

Reading

Assessment objective
- To find and interpret information and ideas (AO1)

Assessment links
English Language Paper 1 questions 1 and 2, and Paper 2 questions 1, 2, 4 and 5

Texts
The extracts for analysis in this unit should be downloaded and printed from the Active Teach Library (see page v) so that they can be read in full and annotated.

1.1 Interpreting text: inference and deduction

Fiction writers present surface facts and events in their stories to inform readers. This is called explicit* information.

They also expect their readers to use inference* and deduction* to find out information that is not on the surface. Readers must reach conclusions based on noticing hints and clues below the surface of the text. This is called implicit* information. We sometimes describe this as 'reading between the lines'.

Skilful readers might argue that this helps them to do this in real life, and be quick to read hints and suggestions in people's speech and behaviour.

 Extract from *Tom Brown's School Days* by Thomas Hughes

Read the extract below from the novel *Tom Brown's School Days*, set in a boarding school in the 1830s. The main character, Tom, has discovered one boy bullying another. Tom stands up to the bully, which leads to a fight.

> 'There's going to be a fight between Slogger Williams and Tom Brown!'
>
> The news ran like wildfire about, and many boys who were on their way to tea at their several houses turned back, and sought the back of the chapel, where the fights come off.

Explicit information about who will be fighting — (annotation for first line)

Implicit information that suggests the news caused excitement — (annotation for second paragraph)

English terms

*Explicit: Expressed directly and with no possibility of confusion

*Inference: An idea or piece of information that a writer suggests, but does not state clearly or explicitly. It can be referred to as 'reading between the lines'.

*Deduction: Drawing a conclusion based on general principles or evidence

*Implicit: Suggested rather than expressed directly

1.1 Interpreting text: inference and deduction

Activity 1

With a partner, discuss how you can tell the difference between explicit and implicit information. Can you find a second example of explicit information in the extract above?

Now read the next section of the story.

> 'Just run and tell East to come and back me,' said Tom to a small School-house boy, who was off like a rocket to Harrowell's, just stopping for a moment to poke his head into the School-house hall, where the lower boys were already at tea, and sing out, 'Fight! Tom Brown and Slogger Williams.'
>
> Up start half the boys at once, leaving bread, eggs, butter, sprats*, and all the rest to take care of themselves. The greater part of the remainder follow in a minute, after swallowing their tea, carrying their food in their hands to consume as they go. Three or four only remain, who steal the butter of the more impetuous*, and make to themselves an unctuous* feast.

In this passage, the writer relies on readers reading between the lines to understand the feelings and motivations of the boys.

Glossary

*Sprats: Small fish that can be eaten

*Impetuous (of a person): Acting quickly without thinking

*Unctuous: Greasy

Examiner tip

Do not worry if you see words in the extract you do not know. This should not stop you completing the question.

Activity 2

Complete the tasks below, using your own words to demonstrate your skills of implicit reading. The first example is done for you.

1. What does the phrase 'Tell East to come and back me' imply about how Tom feels?

   The word 'tell' suggests that Tom feels superior to the small boy as he orders him to go to East. The phrase 'come and back me' suggests that Tom might feel vulnerable or he knows he is not strong enough to deal with the situation of the fight on his own so he asks for another boy to help him.

2. What could the phrase 'off like a rocket' imply about how the small School-house boy feels? Can you give more than one suggestion?

3. What does the phrase 'carrying their food in their hands to consume as they go' imply about the boys' feelings about the fight?

4. What does the writer suggest about the boys who remain in the hall by the phrase 'make to themselves an unctuous feast'?

1 Understanding and interpreting meaning

English term

*Textual evidence: Information you have found in a text to support a specific point

1.2 Selecting textual evidence

To analyse fiction texts, you must be able to pinpoint textual evidence* that supports your conclusions in your reading. Sometimes, this will be straightforward factual evidence; at other times, it will support your inferences. You will usually need to select a short phrase or sentence to illustrate a point, rather than copying out large chunks of quotation.

Considering an example

Read the next section of *Tom Brown's School Days* before completing Activity 3.

> In another minute East and Martin tear through the quadrangle*, carrying a sponge, and arrive at the scene of action just as the combatants are beginning to strip.
>
> Tom felt he had got his work cut out for him, as he stripped off his jacket, waistcoat, and braces. East tied his handkerchief round his waist, and rolled up his shirtsleeves for him. 'Now, old boy, don't you open your mouth to say a word, or try to help yourself a bit—we'll do all that; you keep all your breath and strength for the Slogger.' Martin meanwhile folded the clothes, and put them under the chapel rails; and now Tom, with East to handle him, and Martin to give him a knee, steps out on the turf, and is ready for all that may come; and here is the Slogger too, all stripped, and thirsting for the fray*.

Glossary

*Quadrangle: A courtyard surrounded by a building or several buildings

*Fray: A fight or argument

8

1.2 Selecting textual evidence

Activity 3

Read through the tasks below. Decide which of the suggested quotations is the best choice. You must check:

- whether the quotation proves the statement
- whether the selection contains all the information needed
- whether the quotation matches any instructions in the question. For example that you must choose a word, a phrase* or a sentence* as the answer.

Notice the red underlining on each task. Use this technique of underlining to keep focused on what the task is asking you to do.

1. Copy out <u>the phrase or sentence</u> that identifies the moment when <u>East and Martin arrive</u>.

   Selection 1 In another minute

   Selection 2 just as the combatants are beginning to strip

   Selection 3 In another minute East and Martin tear through the quadrangle, carrying a sponge, and arrive at the scene of action just as the combatants are beginning to strip.

2. Identify <u>the sentence</u> that describes <u>how Tom prepared for his role in the fight</u>.

   Selection 1 Tom felt he had got his work cut out for him, as he stripped off his jacket, waistcoat, and braces.

   Selection 2 he stripped off his jacket, waistcoat, and braces

   Selection 3 East tied his handkerchief round his waist, and rolled up his shirtsleeves for him.

3. Select <u>the word or phrase</u> which suggests that Martin is a well-organised boy.

   Selection 1 folded the clothes

   Selection 2 Martin meanwhile folded the clothes, and put them under the chapel rails

   Selection 3 put

4. Once you have completed tasks 1–3, write an explanation for why you have chosen each word, phrase or sentence.

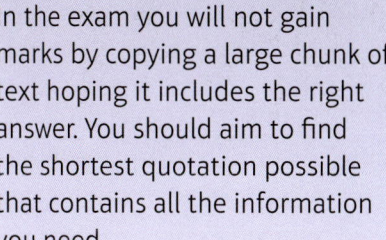

Examiner tip

In the exam you will not gain marks by copying a large chunk of text hoping it includes the right answer. You should aim to find the shortest quotation possible that contains all the information you need.

English terms

*__Phrase:__ A sequence of two or more words arranged in a grammatical construction and acting as a unit in a sentence

*__Sentence:__ A set of words that is complete in itself. It can be identified as beginning with a capital letter and ending with a final punctuation mark such as a full stop, question mark, or exclamation mark.

1 Understanding and interpreting meaning

1.3 Securing your skills

Having compared the different quotations in Activity 3, you should know how to select the best quotation for the question asked. In order to apply these skills, read the next section of the text, where the two boys involved in the fight are described.

> It doesn't look a fair match at first glance: Williams is nearly two inches taller, and probably a long year older than his opponent, and he is very strongly made about the arms and shoulders—'peels well', as the little knot of big fifth-form boys, the amateurs, say, who stand outside the ring of little boys, looking complacently on, but taking no active part in the proceedings. But down below he is not so good by any means—no spring from the loins, and feeblish, not to say shipwrecky, about the knees. Tom, on the contrary, though not half so strong in the arms, is good all over, straight, hard, and springy, from neck to ankle, better perhaps in his legs than anywhere. Besides, you can see by the clear white of his eye, and fresh, bright look of his skin, that he is in tip-top training, able to do all he knows; while the Slogger looks rather sodden, as if he didn't take much exercise and ate too much tuck*. The time-keeper is chosen, a large ring made, and the two stand up opposite one another for a moment, giving us time just to make our little observations.

Glossary
*Tuck: Snack food

Activity 4

Find quotations in the text to support the tasks below.

1. Give two ways in which the writer describes Slogger Williams as physically better than Tom.

2. Identify the phrase which shows the older boys just watch the fight without being involved.

3. Copy out a word which suggests that Tom might do well in the fight.

4. Write out a phrase which suggests that Slogger Williams leads an unhealthy life.

1.3 Securing your skills

Paraphrasing

As well as using quotations, you can also show your understanding of a text by putting it into your own words. This is called paraphrasing. It involves changing the author's choice of words to your own, without changing the original meaning.

Activity 5

Read the following sentences about *Tom Brown's School Days*, which use quotations to explain the events of the text. Then rewrite the sentences, changing the quotations into your own words. Be careful not to change the original meaning. The first example is done for you.

1. Question: How do the younger boys know there is going to be a fight?

   The younger boys know there is going to be a fight because the young boy is described 'just stopping for a moment to poke his head into the School-house hall' to tell them.

   The younger boys know there is going to be a fight because the young boy is described quickly looking into the hall to tell them as he runs past.

2. Question: How does the text suggest that Slogger Williams is physically weak?

   The text suggests that Williams is physically weak by mentioning that 'down below he is not so good by any means'.

   The text suggests that …

3. Question: The text describes the boys taking on various roles in the fight, including the audience and the fighters. What is the third role mentioned?

   The text describes a third role in the scene when it is mentioned that 'the time-keeper is chosen'.

   The text describes …

11

Mini Assessment

Assessment objective

- To find and interpret information and ideas (AO1)

Glossary

*****Condescend:** Lowers himself

*****Partisans:** Supporters

The skills you have secured in this section focus on finding and interpreting information and ideas.

The assessment below will allow you to test your skills and review your progress in preparation for exam-focused work in Section 5 of this book.

Read through the final section of the extract from *Tom Brown's School Days* and complete the tasks which follow.

> 'If Tom'll only condescend* to fight with his head and heels,' as East mutters to Martin, 'we shall do.'
>
> But seemingly he won't, for there he goes in, making play with both hands. Hard all is the word; the two stand to one another like men; rally follows rally in quick succession, each fighting as if he thought to finish the whole thing out of hand. 'Can't last at this rate,' say the knowing ones, while the partisans* of each make the air ring with their shouts and counter-shouts of encouragement, approval, and defiance.
>
> 'Take it easy, take it easy; keep away; let him come after you,' implores East, as he wipes Tom's face after the first round with a wet sponge, while he sits back on Martin's knee, supported by the Madman's long arms which tremble a little from excitement.
>
> 'Time's up,' calls the time-keeper.

1. Which two phrases suggest that Tom is not fighting in the way East would want him to?

2. Select a phrase that describes the onlookers to the fight as noisy.

3. East has clear ideas about how Tom should fight. Use your own words to summarise his advice.

4. Select a word that suggests East cares very much about the outcome of the fight.

Mini Assessment

Self-assessment

Look back at the work you have done in this unit. You can now review your performance of the skills you have practised using *Tom Brown's School Days*.

The skills of AO1 are specifically tested in Paper 1 questions 1 and 2, and Paper 2 questions 1, 2, 4 and 5. However, understanding the implicit and explicit meanings in fiction, together with selecting quotations accurately, is important across the whole reading section of Paper 1.

Skill	🟢 🟠 🔴
I can understand and locate explicit information in a text.	
I can understand and locate implicit information in a text.	
I can select brief quotations from prose fiction in response to a given question.	
I can provide information in my reading answer that is in line with the question asked.	

2 The writer at work: language

Reading

Assessment objective
- Explain, comment on and analyse how writers use language and structure (AO2)

Assessment links
English Language Paper 1 question 3 and Paper 2 question 3

English terms
*Purpose: The overall aim of a text

*Impact: The effect that the writer wants the text to have on the reader

Texts
The extracts for analysis in this unit should be downloaded and printed from the Active Teach Library (see page v) so that they can be read in full and annotated.

2.1 Identifying the writer's purpose

Writers choose the language they use very carefully because it can help them to achieve their intended purpose*. This is the overall aim of the text, and the impact* and effect that writers want it to have on the reader.

Before you start to think about the writer's choice of language, you need to identify the writer's purpose.

Activity 1

1. Look at the different types of text below. Each one has at least one purpose – and may have two or more. What purpose or purposes does each text have? Choose from the words below. The first one has been done to help you.

A An **instruction leaflet** for a new vacuum cleaner.

B A **short story** about a man who spends a night in a haunted house.

C A **newspaper article** in which the writer suggests that meat production is cruel.

D A **non-fiction book** in which the writer talks about his experience climbing Mount Everest.

argue · persuade · inform · explain · describe · advise · entertain

A. instruction leaflet: inform, explain, advise

2. Look again at the four types of text above. Match each one with the impacts that the writer might want their text to have on their audience: the reader. The first one has been done to help you.

- To create a vivid image in the reader's mind
- To change the reader's attitudes or actions
- To create sympathy in the reader
- To interest and engage the reader
- To build a feeling of tension in the reader
- To create a sense of fear in the reader
- To help the reader clearly understand

A. instruction leaflet: to help the reader clearly understand

2.1 Identifying the writer's purpose

 Extract 1 from *Martin Chuzzlewit* by Charles Dickens

Below is an extract from *Martin Chuzzlewit* by Charles Dickens. In the extract, the narrator is describing two characters travelling through a stormy night in a carriage.

The thunder rolled, the lightning flashed; the rain poured down like Heaven's wrath. Surrounded at one moment by intolerable* light, and at the next by pitchy darkness, they still pressed forward on their journey. Even when they arrived at the end of the stage, and might have tarried*, they did not; but ordered horses out immediately. Nor had this any reference to some five minutes' lull, which at that time seemed to promise a cessation* of the storm. They held their course as if they were impelled and driven by its fury. Although they had not exchanged a dozen words, and might have tarried very well, they seemed to feel, by joint consent, that onward they must go.

Activity 2

1. How would you describe the writer's purpose and the impact he wants to have on the reader in this section of the story? Complete the sentences below. You could use one or more of the ideas from Activity 1 to help you – or use your own ideas.

   - I think the writer's purpose in this section of the story is to…
   - The impact the writer wants to have on his reader is…
   - The writer does this by…

2. Choose one sentence or part of a sentence from the extract that helped you to identify the writer's purpose and the impact he wanted to have on the reader. Write a sentence or two explaining how it helped you.

Glossary

*__Intolerable:__ Unbearable

*__Tarried:__ Delayed leaving

*__Cessation:__ Coming to an end

Examiner tip

Ask yourself the following questions to help determine the purpose of a piece of writing.

1. What is the writer describing?
2. What impression does the writer want to create of the scene that he is describing?

2 The writer at work: language

2.2 Identifying significant language features

The writer at work: language choices

When you have identified the writer's purpose, and the impact the writer wanted to have on the reader, you need to identify which of the writer's language choices helped them to achieve this. You can then explore the impact and effect of those language choices.

Rich language choices are what make writing effective.

Activity 3

The sentences below are constructed in a similar way. However, key word choices have a very different impact on the reader. Copy out the sentences and identify the nouns, verbs, adverbs and adjectives. These choices make the sentences very different from each other. The first one is done for you.

- The huge dog snarled viciously at the cat.
- The old woman smiled cheerfully at the boy.
- The tall girl laughed loudly at the joke.

Activity 4

In this activity, think about the writer's purpose and the impact it has on you. You will look for rich language choices and use these to explain the effect on the reader.

Extract 2 from *Martin Chuzzlewit* by Charles Dickens

Look at extract 2 from the novel *Martin Chuzzlewit* by Charles Dickens.

> It was one of those hot, silent nights, when people sit at windows listening for the thunder which they know will shortly break; when they recall dismal tales of hurricanes and earthquakes; and of lonely travellers on open plains, and lonely ships at sea, struck by lightning. Lightning flashed and quivered on the black horizon even now; and hollow murmurings were in the wind, as though it had been blowing where the thunder rolled, and still was charged with its exhausted echoes. But the storm, though gathering swiftly, had not yet come up; and the prevailing* stillness was the more solemn, from the dull* intelligence* that seemed to hover in the air, of noise and conflict afar off.

Glossary

*Prevailing: Existing at a particular time

*Dull: Quiet or muffled

*Intelligence: News or information

2.2 Identifying significant language features

Think about the writer's purpose and the impact it has on you, the reader. Use some of the suggestions below, or your own ideas, to complete these sentences.

1. The writer creates the impression that the storm is…

   distant   dangerous   threatening   violent   powerful   loud   frightening

2. The rich language choices that most strongly suggest this are…

   hot   silent   dismal   flashed   quivered   murmurings

   rolled   solemn   noise   conflict   black

Activity 5

Extract 3 from *Martin Chuzzlewit* by Charles Dickens

Now look at extract 3 from *Martin Chuzzlewit* by Charles Dickens.

It was very dark; but in the murky sky there were masses of cloud which shone with a lurid* light, like monstrous heaps of copper that had been heated in a furnace, and were growing cold. These had been advancing steadily and slowly, but they were now motionless, or nearly so. As the carriage clattered round the corners of the streets, it passed at every one a knot of persons who had come there—many from their houses close at hand, without hats—to look up at that quarter of the sky. And now a very few large drops of rain began to fall, and thunder rumbled in the distance.

Glossary
*Lurid: Bright, unpleasant light

1. How would you sum up the writer's purpose in this extract? What impression of the weather is he trying to create?
2. Which words or phrases in the extract make the most powerful contribution to this purpose? Choose two or three.
3. Write one or two sentences explaining each of your choices.

2 The writer at work: language

English terms

*Onomatopoeia: A word that sounds like the sound it represents (for example, 'crash', 'bang', 'whoosh', etc.)

*Simile: A comparison made using 'like' or 'as' (for example, 'My father ran like a charging rhinoceros.')

*Metaphor: A direct comparison made without using 'like' or 'as' (for example, 'My father was a charging rhinoceros.')

*Personification: Describing something that is not human using language associated with humans (for example, 'The grass whispered and the leaves danced in the breeze.')

*Alliteration: When two or more words positioned close to each other begin with the same sound (for example, 'The grass grew green.')

*Emotive language: Powerful word choices which influence the reader's emotional response

2.3 Commenting on the effect of language

The writer at work: language devices

Language devices used in a text can help you to analyse the writer's choices, but you need to identify them and, more importantly, comment in detail on their effects.

Language devices you can look for in a text include:

- **figurative language**, which can be used to make a comparison creating a vivid visual image in the reader's mind
- devices which use the **sound** of the words to add to their impact on the reader.

The most common language devices you will encounter are onomatopoeia*; similes*; metaphors*; personification*; and alliteration*.

Activity 6

1. Which of the language devices listed in the *English terms* box on the left are examples of figurative language and which are examples of devices linked with sound? Copy the table below. Choose two devices to add to each column.

Figurative language devices	Language devices which link with sound

2. The sentences below are taken from three different texts. What language devices are used in each extract?

A
In the small hours of the morning the river is silent, alone with itself, slapping and sucking at the foreshore beneath my balcony.

Taking the plunge

B
...she shot a few whispered words of broken English at me, her eyes glancing back, like those of a frightened horse, into the gloom behind her.

The Adventure of the Engineer's Thumb

C
Lightning flashed and quivered on the black horizon even now; and hollow murmurings were in the wind.

Martin Chuzzlewit

2.3 Commenting on the effect of language

 Extract from *The Adventure of the Engineer's Thumb* by Arthur Conan Doyle

This short story features the detective Sherlock Holmes. In the story, Sherlock Holmes investigates a strange happening in which an engineer's thumb is cut off.

It was pitch dark inside the house, and the colonel fumbled about looking for matches and muttering under his breath. Suddenly a door opened at the other end of the passage, and a long, golden bar of light shot out in our direction. It grew broader, and a woman appeared with a lamp in her hand, which she held above her head, pushing her face forward and peering at us. I could see that she was pretty, and from the gloss with which the light shone upon her dark dress I knew that it was a rich material. She spoke a few words in a foreign tongue in a tone as though asking a question, and when my companion answered in a gruff monosyllable she gave such a start that the lamp nearly fell from her hand. Colonel Stark went up to her, whispered something in her ear, and then, pushing her back into the room from whence she had come, he walked towards me again with the lamp in his hand.

I glanced at the books upon the table, and in spite of my ignorance of German I could see that two of them were treatises on science*, the others being volumes of poetry. Then I walked across to the window, hoping that I might catch some glimpse of the country-side, but an oak shutter, heavily barred, was folded across it. It was a wonderfully silent house. There was an old clock ticking loudly somewhere in the passage, but otherwise everything was deadly still. A vague feeling of uneasiness began to steal over me. [...]

Suddenly, without any preliminary sound in the midst of the utter stillness, the door of my room swung slowly open. The woman was standing in the aperture*, the darkness of the hall behind her, the yellow light from my lamp beating upon her eager and beautiful face. I could see at a glance that she was sick with fear, and the sight sent a chill to my own heart. She held up one shaking finger to warn me to be silent, and she shot a few whispered words of broken English at me, her eyes glancing back, like those of a frightened horse, into the gloom behind her.

Activity 7

1. Read the first paragraph. To identify the device the writer has used and its impact on the reader, rewrite the sentence below using your own words and a quotation*.

   > The writer uses a metaphor to describe the power and brightness of the light.

2. Now read the rest of the extract. How has the writer used language devices to interest readers in the setting and characters? Write one or two paragraphs to explain your ideas using quotations from the text. Comment on the writer's use of alliteration and simile.

Glossary

*Treatises on science:** Books exploring or explaining scientific ideas

*Aperture:** An opening

English term

*Quotation:** A group of words taken from a text and copied exactly as they appeared in the text

2 The writer at work: language

2.4 Using evidence

When you analyse the writer's use of language in a text, you need to support your ideas with relevant quotations from the text.

Activity 8

The most effective quotations are short, relevant and focused: you only need to select the word, phrase or sentence that supports your point.

1. Look at the quotations below. They are taken from *The Adventure of the Engineer's Thumb*. Which quotation would you choose to support this point: **the writer suggests that the mysterious woman is frightened?**

    A 'She held up one shaking finger to warn me to be silent, and she shot a few whispered words of broken English at me'

    B 'She held up one shaking finger to warn me to be silent'

    C 'She held up one shaking finger'

    D 'one shaking finger'

2. Is your chosen quotation fully relevant to, and focused on, the point it is supporting? Write one or two sentences explaining your choice.

You can use much shorter quotations, and include two or three that support the same point, by embedding them in your response. 'Embedding them' means they are part of the flow of your argument within a sentence and are not quoted on their own. For example: The writer shows that the narrator is frightened because seeing the mysterious woman sent 'a chill' to his heart.

Activity 9

Choose two short, relevant quotations from this extract to complete the sentence below, giving evidence for the statement that the writer is suggesting the woman is frightened. Aim to embed your chosen quotations.

> She held up one shaking finger to warn me to be silent, and she shot a few whispered words of broken English at me, her eyes glancing back, like those of a frightened horse, into the gloom behind her.

The writer suggests the woman is frightened, describing .... and ....

Examiner tip

Remember, when you use a quotation, enclose it in quotation marks and make sure you copy it accurately from the text.

Examiner tip

Make sure you only choose words and phrases from within the line range given in the question.

This quotation is not embedded:	These quotations are embedded:
The narrator describes the mysterious woman as frightened: 'I could see at a glance that she was sick with fear'.	The narrator says he 'could see at a glance' that the mysterious woman was 'sick with fear'.

2.4 Using evidence

Activity 10

Look again at this extract from *The Adventure of the Engineer's Thumb*.

I glanced at the books upon the table, and in spite of my ignorance of German I could see that two of them were treatises on science, the others being volumes of poetry. Then I walked across to the window, hoping that I might catch some glimpse of the country-side, but an oak shutter, heavily barred, was folded across it. It was a wonderfully silent house. There was an old clock ticking loudly somewhere in the passage, but otherwise everything was deadly still. A vague feeling of uneasiness began to steal over me.

1. How would you describe the mood the writer creates in this part of the text? Choose one or two of the words below, or use your own ideas.

   tense   disturbing   joyful   dramatic   mysterious

   exciting   frightening   comical

2. Which of these quotations fully support your chosen ideas? Choose two.

   A   I glanced at the books upon the table
   B   I walked across to the window
   C   an oak shutter, heavily barred, was folded across it
   D   a wonderfully silent house
   E   an old clock ticking loudly
   F   everything was deadly still
   G   A vague feeling of uneasiness began to steal over me.

3. Write two or three sentences, exploring how the writer uses language to create atmosphere or mood in the extract. Aim to:
   - use short, relevant, focused quotations
   - embed your chosen quotations in your response.

> **Examiner tip**
> Comment on quotations and analyse the effect of language and techniques.

21

2 The writer at work: language

English term

*****Word class:** A category of word that defines the function the word has in a sentence. Categories include noun, verb, adjective, adverb, pronoun, etc.

2.5 Using terminology

Terminology is very important. When you comment on one of the writer's language choices, aim to identify its word class*. This may reveal a significant pattern in the writer's choices, for example an effect the writer has achieved through their choice of verbs.

Activity 11

1. Remind yourself of the definitions of the different word classes. Copy the table and add the definitions below. Then think of some examples to include. Some of the table has been completed to help you.

   describes a noun   replaces or stands in for a noun

   connects words, phrases, clauses or sentences

   identifies an object, place, person or idea   identifies an action, event or state

Word class	Definition	Examples
noun		
verb		
adjective		
adverb	describes a verb, modifies an adjective	
conjunction		and, but, because, if
pronoun		

Examiner tip

Learning subject terminology will help you to write about the effect of the writer's craft.

2. Look at this extract from *The Adventure of the Engineer's Thumb*. Copy and complete the student's comment below by adding the correct word classes. Use the table above to help you.

   There was an old clock ticking loudly somewhere in the passage, but otherwise everything was deadly still.

   The writer creates a tense atmosphere or mood, describing the house using the _____ 'still', emphasising it with the _____ 'deadly'. This focuses the reader on the tension-building ticking of the clock, which the writer highlights with the _____ 'loudly'.

2.5 Using terminology

Activity 12

Look again at extract 2 from *Martin Chuzzlewit*.

It was one of those <u>hot, silent</u> nights, when people sit at windows listening for the thunder which they know will shortly break; when they recall <u>dismal</u> tales of hurricanes and earthquakes; and of <u>lonely</u> travellers on open plains, and <u>lonely</u> ships at sea, struck by lightning.

1. What do the two underlined adjectives in the first part of the sentence suggest about the night on which this part of the story takes place? Write one or two sentences explaining your ideas. You could use the suggestions below to help you, or use your own ideas.

   miserable   disturbing   tense   unsettling   danger   threat

2. How do the other underlined adjectives in the sentence contribute to the mood? Write one or two sentences explaining your ideas. You could use the suggestions above to help you, or use your own ideas.

3. Now look again at part of extract 1 from *Martin Chuzzlewit*.

   The thunder (rolled), the lightning flashed; the rain poured down like Heaven's wrath.

   a. Identify the verbs that the writer has used in this sentence. The first one has been done for you.

   b. What do the verbs suggest about the storm? Write one or two sentences explaining your ideas.

2 The writer at work: language

2.6 Exploring the effect of language

When you identify a significant language choice in a text, you can develop your comments by explaining the ideas, thoughts or feelings that it suggests. It is important to use your skills of analysis to consider the effect of the writer's language choices on the reader.

Connotation

> **English term**
>
> *Connotation: An idea, feeling or impression that a word or phrase creates in the reader's mind

Writers often make a specific language choice because of the connotations* of a word or phrase. It is helpful to consider the ideas, or connotations, that a language choice creates in your mind when commenting on its effect.

Activity 13

 Extract from 'Taking the plunge' by Matthew Parris.

Now look at the opening part of the extract taken from the newspaper article 'Taking the plunge' by Matthew Parris.

I have been thinking, talking, and finally fretting about swimming across the River Thames for 15 years since, in my forties, I moved into a flat on Narrow Street in the East End of London, looking out over the river at Limehouse Reach. I watched 20ft tides racing up and down the river. Swans, cormorants, traffic cones and sometimes corpses floated by. Barges, sailing ships, warships, cruise liners, disco boats and police launches buzzed, roared or chugged past my balcony, day and night.

1. Look at the spidergrams below, showing some of the connotations of two language choices about the river. Copy them and add your own ideas.

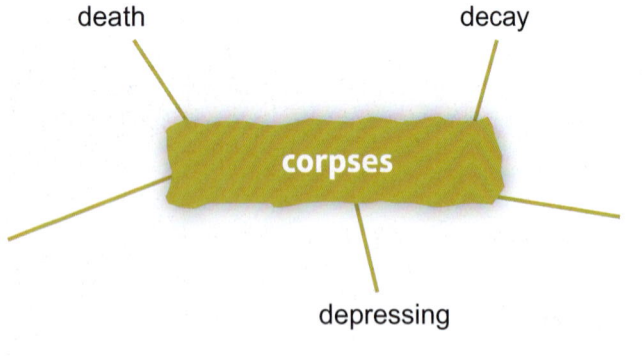
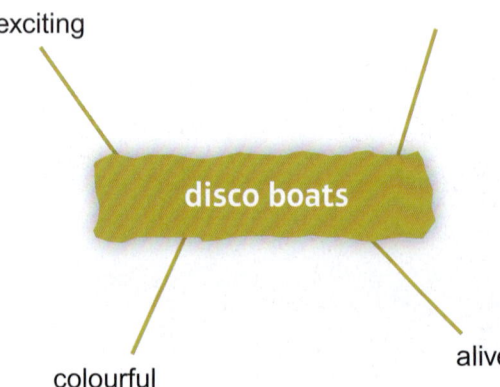

2. What impressions does the word 'corpse' create of the setting of the River Thames? Write a sentence or two, explaining how the connotations of this word contribute to your impressions.

3. What impressions does the phrase 'disco boats' create of the River Thames? Write a sentence or two, explaining how the connotations of this phrase contribute to your impressions.

2.6 Exploring the effect of language

Activity 14

Look at another extract from 'Taking the plunge'.

I'm no great swimmer, but I can stay afloat. I would make my crossing in high summer when the water was warmest, and at high tide, as it turned. I would start from the stairs at Globe Wharf on the other side and swim straight across to the Ratcliff Cross stairs at Narrow Street.

And I would do it without a boat or any kind of flotation in tow, because otherwise it isn't real. I started telling friends of my plan.

But somehow I never got around to executing it. The years passed; I turned 50, then 55. Friends would (yawn) as I insisted that I'd do it. Sometimes someone would say: "How about tonight?" and I'd be momentarily keen, then reflect that the tide wasn't right, I needed to be fresh for the morning … or whatever.

1. What can you infer from the extract about the writer's plans?
2. Create a spidergram to explore the connotations of the circled word in the extract.
3. Write a sentence or two explaining how the connotations of this word contribute to your impressions of the writer's plans.
4. Which other words in the extract contribute to your impression of the writer's plans? Choose one or two, and create spidergrams exploring their connotations.
5. Write a paragraph or two exploring some of the ways in which the writer's use of language in this extract contributes to your impressions of his plans.

25

2 The writer at work: language

English terms

*Mood: The atmosphere or feelings that a text creates for the reader, conveyed through language choice

*Tone: The way a writer expresses a certain attitude or mood through their language choices. This can often help the reader imagine the voice of the narrator or writer.

Examiner tip

Unit 7 covers tone in more detail – see pages 88–89, 7.3 Writing tone.

2.7 Exploring the writer's voice

The writer's language choices throughout a text can contribute to the mood* and tone* of the text. Try to 'hear' the voice of the writer as you read. Consider the tone of their voice and the mood it creates.

Activity 15

Look again at this extract from 'Taking the plunge'.

> I have been thinking, talking, and finally fretting about swimming across the River Thames for 15 years ... But somehow I never got around to executing it. The years passed; I turned 50, then 55. Friends would yawn as I insisted that I'd do it. Sometimes someone would say: "How about tonight?" and I'd be momentarily keen, then reflect that the tide wasn't right, I needed to be fresh for the morning ... or whatever.

1. Think about the different voices in which you could read this extract, then look at the examples below. Which voice would help to create which mood?

A	A cheerful voice…	G	…to create a disturbing mood
B	An anxious voice…	H	…to create a mysterious mood
C	A sarcastic voice…	I	…to create an exciting mood
D	A slow, monotonous voice…	J	…to create a humorous mood
E	A quiet, hesitating voice…	K	…to create a peaceful mood
F	A loud, breathless voice…	L	…to create a tense mood

2. Which two or three different types of voice might suit the extract above?

3. Read the extract aloud, or to yourself, two or three times. Each time you read it, choose one of the different tones of voice you noted in task 2. Which voice **best** suits the text?

4. Now think about how the text, and the writer's use of language, guided your answer to task 3. Note down one or two quotations from the extract that particularly suit the tone of voice you chose.

2.7 Exploring the writer's voice

Matthew Parris

Activity 16

Now look at this extract from 'Taking the plunge'.

> I watched 20ft tides racing up and down the river. Swans, cormorants, traffic cones and sometimes corpses floated by. Barges, sailing ships, warships, cruise liners, disco boats and police launches buzzed, roared or chugged past my balcony, day and night.
>
> Except at my favourite time. In the small hours of the morning the river is silent, alone with itself, slapping and sucking at the foreshore beneath my balcony. This would be the time to swim across, with no shipping and nobody to raise an alarm.

1. How would you describe the mood and tone that the writer creates in each paragraph? You could use some of the suggestions in Activity 15 to help you, or use your own ideas.

2. Note down one or two short quotations from the extract that particularly show the mood and tone you noted in each paragraph.

3. Look closely at each word in the quotations you noted in task 2. Which two or three words or phrases make the most significant contribution to the mood and tone of each paragraph?

4. Write a paragraph or two exploring the mood and tone of this extract. Aim to:
   - identify how the mood changes
   - support your ideas with short, relevant quotations from the text
   - consider how the writer uses language and tone to create the moods you have identified.

27

2 The writer at work: language

English terms

*Purpose: The overall aim of a text

*Impact: The effect that the writer wants the text to have on the reader

2.8 Analysing the writer's choices

You can develop your analysis of the writer's language choices by making a range of different types of comment. You can talk about:

- purpose* (why the writer is writing the piece)
- impact* (how the piece of writing affects the reader)
- inference (what is suggested by the text)
- connotation (the ideas and feelings that the writer creates using different words and phrases).

Think about the following questions when you comment on a writer's choice of word or phrase.

From the writer's choices	To the effect on the reader
What can you work out about the situation or characters from this language choice?	How does this language choice help the writer to achieve their intention?
What ideas does this language choice create in your mind?	What effect does this language choice have on the reader?

Look at this annotated extract from 'Taking the plunge' by Matthew Parris. He has just swum across the River Thames.

suggests that Parris is feeling relief —

I (stopped shivering.) The shower (so much mud!) (was sublime.)
The (sweet tea was nectar.) The sleep was heavenly.

suggests his enjoyment —

suggests extreme pleasure

Activity 17

Look at the three annotations commenting on the writer's language choices in the extract above. What specific language choices have been used for each one? For example, the first annotation comments on inference. Parris does not say he felt relieved, but we can infer that he is from the fact that he 'stopped shivering'.

2.8 Analysing the writer's choices

Activity 18

Now revisit the newspaper article, 'Taking the plunge'. Read this extract.

There's a kind of relief, once you start. The water was choppy but not too cold, and I could feel no current. We swam silently, breaststroke, surprised at the ease. Except that across the water, perspectives were altering unaccountably. Then I saw trees moving behind the buildings on the other side. Why? When I turned to look for the Globe Stairs behind us, they were far over to our right. We were being carried upstream. Fast. The tide was still coming in. Fast.

We decided to stay close together, not to fight the current, and keep swimming towards the opposite bank; hard work now in the choppy water.

1. Write one or two paragraphs exploring how the writer uses language to describe the experience of swimming across the River Thames. Aim to:
   - identify significant language choices
   - comment on what can be inferred from them, and their effect.

2. Annotate your response, labelling where you have commented on:
   - what can be inferred
   - connotations of particular words and phrases
   - the impact or effect on the reader.

2 The writer at work: language

2.9 Writing about language choice

In this section, you will practise identifying significant language choices, and using them to develop an effective analysis of the writer's use of language.

In the exam, you will need to think about all of the ways in which the writer has used language choices to achieve their desired effect.

Thinking about language

Activity 19

Revisit this extract from *The Adventure of the Engineer's Thumb*.

> Suddenly, without any preliminary sound in the midst of the utter stillness, the door of my room swung slowly open. The woman was standing in the aperture, the darkness of the hall behind her, the yellow light from my lamp beating upon her eager and beautiful face. I could see at a glance that she was sick with fear, and the sight sent a chill to my own heart. She held up one shaking finger to warn me to be silent, and she shot a few whispered words of broken English at me, her eyes glancing back, like those of a frightened horse, into the gloom behind her.

1. Copy and complete the table below.

What kind of mood or feeling is the writer trying to create in this section of the text?	What is the effect on the reader?

2. a. Identify three significant words or phrases in the extract that contribute to the intention or mood you noted in task 1.

   b. Use the correct terminology to identify the word class or language device used in each case.

   c. Comment on the effect on the reader.

Activity 20

Look at one student's comments on the writer's use of language in the extract above.

> In this section of the text, the writer suggests a nervous mood. The narrator suggests the woman seems nervous because he describes her as 'sick with fear'. The adjective 'sick' suggests she is so nervous that it is making her ill, or perhaps even killing her. The narrator describes her finger 'shaking' which also suggests she is nervous.

2.9 Writing about language choice

1. What has the student done well?
2. What could the student have done better?
3. Think about the words the student has used to express their ideas.

    a. How many times has the student used the words 'nervous' and 'suggests'?

    b. Rewrite the student's comments, aiming to avoid repetition and to make them as precise as possible. You could use some of the suggestions in the spider diagrams to help you.

4. Use your notes from tasks 1, 2 and 3 to write your own paragraph exploring the writer's use of language in Activity 19.

5. Look at your response to task 4.

    a. Which of the following criteria have you achieved? Annotate your response, labelling at least one example of each criterion.

    - Supported my ideas with relevant, focused evidence
    - Identified significant language choices
    - Used the correct terminology to identify significant word classes or language devices
    - Commented on what can be inferred from the writer's language choices
    - Commented on the connotations, impact and/or effect of the writer's language choices
    - Expressed my ideas precisely, avoiding repetition

    b. Review and revise your response so that you have achieved and labelled each of the criteria above.

Examiner tip

Remember to use PEA (Point, Evidence and Analysis) when responding to a language question in the exam.

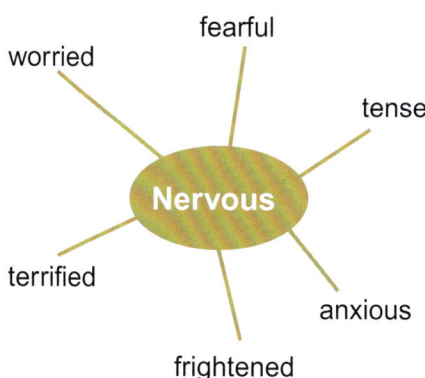

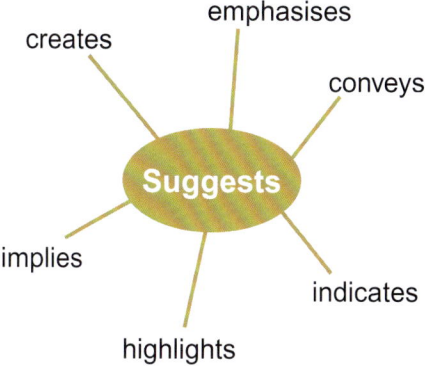

Mini Assessment

Assessment objective
- Explain, comment on and analyse how writers use language and structure (AO2)

The skills you have developed in this unit focus on explaining, commenting on and analysing how writers use language and structure.

The assessments on these two pages will allow you to test your language analysis skills and review your progress in preparation for exam-focused work.

Paper 1, Section A, Reading: 19th-century fiction

Read this extract from *Martin Chuzzlewit* by Charles Dickens, then answer the questions that follow. You will have seen this extract before in this unit.

> The thunder rolled, the lightning flashed; the rain poured down like Heaven's wrath. Surrounded at one moment by intolerable light, and at the next by pitchy darkness, they still pressed forward on their journey. Even when they arrived at the end of the stage, and might have tarried, they did not; but ordered horses out immediately. Nor had this any reference to some five minutes' lull, which at that time seemed to promise a cessation of the storm. They held their course as if they were impelled and driven by its fury. Although they had not exchanged a dozen words, and might have tarried very well, they seemed to feel, by joint consent, that onward they must go.

1. a. Suggest two words or phrases to describe the purpose of this fiction text.

   b. Write down one word that you think summarises the characters' thoughts, feelings and actions.

2. In this passage, the writer tries to convey the tense atmosphere or mood of the storm. Note down three significant language choices the writer has made in order to achieve that intention. They could be words or short phrases.

3. Look again at your response to task 2. Label each of your answers using the correct terminology, for example, 'noun', 'simile', etc.

4. Look again at your response to task 2. Annotate each word or phrase, thinking about its impact on the reader.

5. Choose one of your answers to task 4. Write two or three sentences exploring how this language choice helps the writer to convey the tense atmosphere or mood of the storm. You could use some of the words and phrases in the spider diagram to the left to help you.

Mini Assessment

Paper 2, Section A, Reading: 20th-century non-fiction

Read these final paragraphs of the extract from 'Taking the plunge', a newspaper article by Matthew Parris. Then answer the questions that follow.

> It's being woken in the dark that's worst. I donned trunks and an old singlet to swim in, and some discardable flip-flops. We stood on the balcony. The river was very black. We called a minicab just after 3am to take us under the nearby Rotherhithe Tunnel to the other side. We crept down the Globe Stairs wordlessly, so as not to alert any flat-dwellers, and undressed. Each wondered if he'd be going ahead if it wasn't for the other. [...]
>
> There's a kind of relief, once you start. The water was choppy but not too cold, and I could feel no current. We swam silently, breaststroke, surprised at the ease. Except that across the water, perspectives were altering unaccountably. Then I saw trees moving behind the buildings on the other side. Why? When I turned to look for Globe Stairs behind us, they were far over to our right. We were being carried upstream. Fast. The tide was still coming in. Fast.

1. In this extract, the writer describes swimming across the River Thames at night. What impression does the writer create of the experience? Note down two or three words to describe it.

2. Note down every word and phrase in the extract above that helps to create this impression.

3. Which of the words and phrases you have noted create the strongest impression of the writer's experience? Choose three.

    a. Label the words you chose using the correct terminology.

    b. Annotate the words, noting what they suggest and their impact on the reader.

4. Write a paragraph or two exploring how the writer has used language to describe the experience of swimming across the River Thames.

Self-assessment

Look back at the work you have done in this unit. You can now review your performance on the skills you have practised.

The skills of AO2 are tested in Paper 1 question 3 and Paper 2 question 3.

Skill	🟢 🟠 🔴
I can identify the writer's purpose in a text.	
I can select significant and relevant language choices.	
I can use terminology accurately to identify the writer's language choices in a text.	
I can comment in depth on the writer's language choices, exploring their impact and their effect on the reader.	

3 The writer at work: structure

Reading

Assessment objective
- Explain, comment on and analyse how writers use structure to achieve effects and influence readers, using relevant subject terminology to support their views (AO2)

Assessment links
English Language Paper 1 question 3 and Paper 2 question 3

English term
*Purpose: The overall aim of a text

Texts
The extracts for analysis in this unit should be downloaded and printed from the Active Teach Library (see page v) so that they can be read in full and annotated.

3.1 Understanding and identifying structural features

A writer constructs a text. Think of a text like a building, divided into sections. Each section is planned, has a specific purpose*, and links to the other sections to make up the whole. As a critical reader, you should understand how it is built.

Considering an example

Look at the image below of The Shard in London, together with some quotations from a report on its design and structure.

Activity 1

Discuss how you think the structure of the building meets its purpose as an icon of modern London – a 'vertical city' combining work and leisure.

- What do you learn about the building's sections and organisation?
- What is the purpose (for example, work, leisure, residential, tourism) of each of the marked sections?

VIEWING GALLERY 68 – 72

APARTMENTS 53 – 65

HOTEL 34 – 52

RESTAURANTS & BARS 31 – 33

OFFICES 2 – 28

> The vision for The Shard was to create an architecturally striking vertical city incorporating retail, offices, hotel, apartments, restaurants and a public viewing gallery.

> From the ground up, the offices, restaurants, hotel, residences and viewing galleries coincide to create a 'total' building that offers almost everything a business could need.

> The idea was to create a diverse vibrant community.

> The Shard represents a new approach to expanding the urban landscape. Offices, residences and public spaces alike are all taken skyward.

> Over one 36-hour period – employing 700 lorry-loads, one every three minutes – the team poured 5,400 cubic metres of concrete.

Real Estate Management (UK) Limited

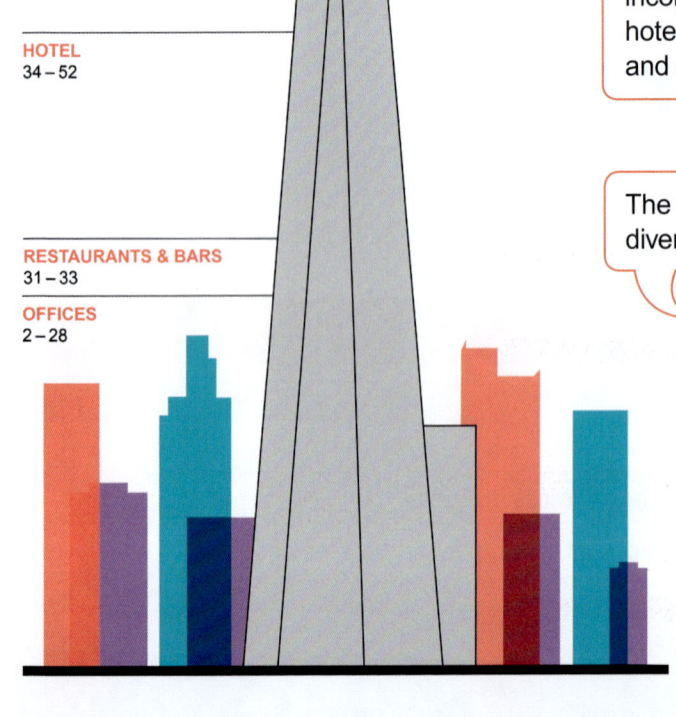

3.1 Understanding and identifying structural features

Like a building, a successful text has an overall shape. It is planned and built in sections. Each section has one or several purposes. Examples of these structural labels are:

- to introduce an idea
- to provide evidence, add detail or give examples
- to establish a turning point, shift or change
- to contrast with a previous idea
- to link or repeat a previous idea
- to conclude.

> **Examiner tip**
>
> When you are asked to look at the structure of a text, think about the effect the author is trying to create and how they do this.

Each section of a skilled piece of writing will link with the others to form the whole and combine with the language features to achieve the writer's aim.

Activity 2

 **'The view from the Shard: is it worth it?' by Jon Henley**

Read the opening words of each paragraph from a short opinion piece about The Shard, from a national newspaper. Notice the way the writer has structured the piece.

Can you predict the correct structural labels for the final two paragraphs by reading the initial sentences only? Use the ideas from the list above to label them.

The view from the Shard: is it worth it?

Paragraph 1: From tomorrow you can…
Answer: To introduce an idea

Paragraph 2: There's a hitch, though…
Answer: To establish a turning point

Paragraph 3: Thankfully, there are less ruinous ways of getting an eyeful of Britain's capital…
Answer:

Paragraph 4: And Parliament Hill (322ft), Primrose Hill (256ft) and Greenwich Hill are all completely free.
Answer:

3 The writer at work: structure

English terms

*Topic sentence: Usually the first sentence in a paragraph which signposts the topic of the text that follows

*Structural shift: A turning point or change in a text, for example in mood, viewpoint or argument in a written text

Glossary

*Acrophobia: Fear of heights

3.2 Identifying shifts and changes

Analysis of the structure of a text requires you to be alert to shifts and changes. The first place to look for this in a non-fiction text is at the beginning of each paragraph: the topic sentence* may help you to pinpoint the focus of what is to follow and identify any changes in topic that build the whole text.

There may also be a specific structural shift* in a text, where significant change occurs. This could be in the mood, argument or focus of the text.

Now read the whole article on The Shard below and notice the annotations identifying the structural features. Check if your assumptions for Activity 2, based on the opening of each paragraph, were accurate.

Headline →

The view from the Shard: is it worth it?

John Henley, *The Guardian*, Thursday 5 July 2012

Lead – the opening sentence or paragraph in a news story that contains the key details →

At almost £25 a ticket to go up western Europe's tallest building, there are cheaper ways to get a view of London.

Introductory paragraph – establishing the facts about The Shard and its opening date →

From tomorrow you can, should acrophobia* not be one of your more pressing fears, book a ticket to the top of western Europe's tallest building. Level 68 of the Shard offers what is by all accounts a fairly mind-blowing 360-degree view of London from 800ft up, plus a vista stretching – assuming the weather ever improves – 40 miles.

Shift or change – the writer establishes a problem, the cost →

There's a hitch, though: tickets cost £24.95 for an adult, and £18.95 for a child, meaning a trip to the top for a family of four will set you back roughly 90 quid. That's a lot more than the €14 (about £11) price of an adult ticket up the Eiffel Tower, even if, as the PR company promoting the Shard helpfully points out, the 'visitor experience' includes a 30-second ride in something called a 'kaleidoscopic lift'.

Contrasting but linked information – the writer establishes a number of cheaper alternatives to The Shard →

Thankfully, there are less ruinous ways of getting an eyeful of Britain's capital. An actual glass of champagne at Tower 42's Vertigo 42 bar, for example, 600ft above Broad Street, is only £14. The Golden Gallery of St Paul's cathedral offers great views of the Thames from 280ft for just £1 more, plus the undeniably virtuous feeling that will come with knowing you've climbed 528 steps to get there. The new 295ft Emirates cable car is a mere £3.20 with an Oyster card.

Final neat link to the opening and main topic →

And Parliament Hill (322ft), Primrose Hill (256ft) and Greenwich Hill are all completely free. Shard? Schmard.

Summary or conclusion

36

3.2 Identifying shifts and changes

Activity 3

Read the full article again, then with a partner:

1. Discuss whether your predictions in Activity 2 were correct.

2. Summarise the content of the article in just one sentence.

3. Identify the purpose(s), audience and text type of the writing, selecting one or two of the most accurate terms from each group below:

Text type: magazine article, obituary, autobiography, biography, newspaper article, travel writing, letter, short story, novel

Audience: young people, the general public, tourists, readers of *The Guardian*, overseas visitors to London, Londoners, holidaymakers

Purpose: to inform, to argue, to persuade, to advise, to describe, to entertain

37

3 The writer at work: structure

> **Examiner tip**
> Try to link structural features in a text to the writer's overall intentions.

3.3 Writing about whole text structure, using terminology and evidence

Once you have understood a text's purpose and construction, you need to be able to write about this analytically. You must explain how structural features contribute to the text's success. Remember to use English language terminology related to structure in your analysis.

Non-fiction

For non-fiction such as letters, newspaper articles and text books, you might identify some of the following structural features:

Headline · Title · Subtitle · Lead · Paragraph · Section · Introduction

Conclusion · Text box · Salutation and closing · Caption · Beginning

- The writer shifts the focus of his argument on to readers' experiences in **paragraph 7**...
- **Line 5** of the letter marks a change from introduction to the key point of argument.
- **The subtitle** of the obituary conveys the writer's viewpoint and contradicts the commonly-held view of the subject.
- The text shifts with **the word 'however'**, as the writer provides a different point of view.

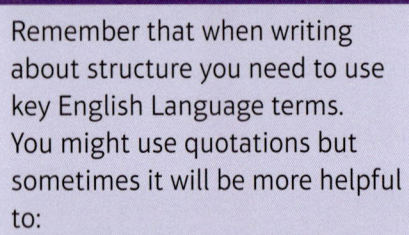

> **Examiner tip**
> Remember that when writing about structure you need to use key English Language terms. You might use quotations but sometimes it will be more helpful to:
> - use line references
> - indicate a paragraph number
> - use a structural term such as 'conclusion' or 'headline'.

Prose fiction

Most prose fiction texts you come across for GCSE English Language will be extracts from conventional short stories or novels. Which of the terms in the coloured boxes, commonly used for non-fiction, might you also use for fiction?

Activity 4

This activity is based on the first paragraphs of a student answer about the overall structure of the text about The Shard on page 39. Read the student answer to the question below, then complete the following tasks.

> 'Analyse how the writer has structured his text to convey his argument effectively.'

1. Identify the key English Language terminology used by the student to identify structural features.

2. Identify where the candidate has used quotations, paragraph numbers, line references or structural terms to pinpoint supporting evidence for the points made.

3. Add a final paragraph that comments on the conclusion of 'The view from the Shard' on page 36. Remember to use appropriate terminology.

3.3 Writing about whole text structure, using terminology and evidence

The writer of this opinion piece argues that the newly opening Shard is over-priced for visitors.

He uses the headline of the article 'The View from the Shard: is it worth it?' to introduce his point of view, that the Shard is too expensive. The lead then provides further support for this by highlighting details of price and that there are better choices than going to the Shard.

The introductory paragraph establishes the topic of the opening of the Shard and gives information about the overall experience of the Shard and the views of London. However, the piece soon changes by the first line of paragraph two with the phrase 'There's a hitch though'. This establishes a shift of focus and changes the writing from information about the Shard to a negative viewpoint about it as the writer goes on to talk about the price.

The penultimate paragraph provides a contrast with paragraph one and explores the alternatives to the Shard, giving linked information on the topic of high buildings. The writer argues that these choices are 'less ruinous ways of getting an eyeful of Britain's capital'. He uses information about these other cheaper places to convey his argument that the Shard is not the best choice.

> **Examiner tip**
>
> Notice how the student moves from the beginning to the end of the text logically, analysing the structure chronologically.

3 The writer at work: structure

3.4 Identifying sentence types

Whole text structure refers to the way a text is organised in sections that relate to each other and create a complete piece of writing. It is also concerned with the way individual sentences and punctuation are used by the writer to build the text.

Activity 5

Remind yourself of some of the terminology you might use to comment on sentences and punctuation. Can you match each term below with the correct definition?

A Minor sentence **B** Single clause sentence **C** Multi-clause sentence

D Rhetorical question **E** Quotation **F** Short sentence

G Long sentence **H** List **I** Ellipsis

1. Sometimes called a simple sentence. It contains a subject and one finite verb.

2. Sometimes called a compound or complex sentence. It contains more than one clause – each of which will have a subject and a finite verb. It is made up of two or more finite verbs.

3. A sentence which, in comparison to those surrounding it, is extended in length.

4. A question that is asked for emphasis or effect where no answer is expected from the audience or reader.

5. Strictly speaking this is not a sentence, but the term is commonly used to describe a short sentence fragment which conveys meaning and is punctuated as a sentence.

6. A sentence which, in comparison to those surrounding it, is brief in length.

7. Evidence from another source, which is included and acknowledged using inverted commas.

8. A grouping of items or names written consecutively and divided by commas or semi colons. This may be introduced by a colon.

9. The punctuation '…' marking a pause or incompleteness.

3.4 Identifying sentence types

Activity 6

Read the sentences below taken from 'The view from the Shard.' The writer uses various sentence forms to strengthen the critical tone of his piece and give information and opinion.

1. Decide which of the terms from Activity 5 best describes each sentence below.

2. Which of the sentences below are used to convey information in the text? Give reasons for your answers.

3. Which of the sentences below do you think are used to convey the writer's critical viewpoint and tone about The Shard? Give reasons for your answers.

> That's a lot more than the €14 (about £11) price of an adult ticket up the Eiffel Tower, even if, as the PR company promoting The Shard helpfully points out, the 'visitor experience' includes a 30-second ride in something called a 'kaleidoscopic lift'.

> From tomorrow you can, should acrophobia not be one of your more pressing fears, book a ticket to the top of western Europe's tallest building.

> The new 295ft Emirates cable car is a mere £3.20 with an Oyster card.

> Shard? Schmard.

Activity 7

Look back at the student answer in Activity 4 on page 39. You now have enough information to write a final paragraph of your own about the writer's use of sentence structures, in answer to the question:

> 'Analyse how the writer has used a variety of sentence structures to convey his argument effectively.'

Complete the paragraph below to convey what you know about the writer's use of sentence structures in 'The view from the Shard'. Remember to use appropriate terminology.

> In addition, the writer uses a range of sentence structures to convey his argument effectively. He opens the piece with a multi-clause sentence and uses the sub-clause 'should acrophobia not be one of your more pressing fears' to emphasise a rather negative argument about The Shard since it suggests the negative aspect to any trip up the building....

3 The writer at work: structure

3.5 Structuring fiction

You will now apply what you have learned about structure to a fiction text, which also focuses on an unusual building and its astonishing view: an extract from the novel, *Dracula*, by Bram Stoker.

The usual aim of a fiction writer is to entertain and engage a reader in the imaginative world of the story. To achieve this, a writer may structure a text using **characters**, **time**, **perspective** and **setting**.

Characters and relationships	Time
The writer must support the reader in understanding the thoughts, feelings and relationships of the characters. The combination or positioning of characters may emphasise contrast* or parallels*. Sections of **dialogue** (direct or reported speech*), **action** and **reaction** may structure a text.	The writer must help readers to understand the order of events and any previous or future events that might be relevant to what is being described. A text might be structured: • in chronological order* • alternating between two time periods • containing flashbacks to previous times • containing predictions or foreshadowing* of future events.
Perspective: big picture versus small detail	**Setting**
The structure of a text often works rather like a camera, **zooming in to focus on particular details** or **zooming out to consider the wider setting**, to focus the reader's view on particular aspects of setting, character and action.	A text may be structured by moving from one setting to another, for example, from inside to outside, from one room to another, from one building to another. Such settings might emphasise contrast or parallels.

English terms

*Contrast: Using two opposite ideas

*Parallel: Using two similar ideas

*Direct speech: The exact words spoken by a person, using speech marks and followed by a reporting verb such as 'said', or 'cried'

*Reported speech: A report of what someone said, not using their exact words

*Chronological order: In time order from beginning to end

*Foreshadow: Predict

Zooming out to consider the wider setting

Zooming in to focus on particular details

3.6 Identifying structural choices

Read and understand the whole text before you begin work.

Extract from *Dracula* by Bram Stoker

Read the following extract from the novel, *Dracula*. The narrator, Jonathan Harker, is staying in Count Dracula's castle. In this diary extract, he thinks back to his arrival at the castle and what he learns about his host, Count Dracula. He considers the effect the place is having on him now. The passage begins with his memory of his conversation with Count Dracula.

> **Glossary**
>
> *****Haste:** Speed
>
> *****Tell on me:** To have a negative effect on me
>
> *****Start:** To be frightened by

'... let me warn you with all seriousness, that should you leave these rooms you will not by any chance go to sleep in any other part of the castle. It is old, and has many memories, and there are bad dreams for those who sleep unwisely. Be warned! Should sleep now or ever overcome you, or be like to do, then haste* to your own chamber or to these rooms, for your rest will then be safe. But if you be not careful in this respect, then,' He finished his speech in a gruesome way, for he motioned with his hands as if he were washing them. I quite understood. My only doubt was as to whether any dream could be more terrible than the unnatural, horrible net of gloom and mystery which seemed closing around me.

When he left me I went to my room. After a little while, not hearing any sound, I came out and went up the stone stair to where I could look out towards the South. There was some sense of freedom in the vast expanse, inaccessible though it was to me, as compared with the narrow darkness of the courtyard. Looking out on this, I felt that I was indeed in prison, and I seemed to want a breath of fresh air, though it were of the night. I am beginning to feel this nocturnal existence tell on me*. It is destroying my nerve. I start* at my own shadow, and am full of all sorts of horrible imaginings. God knows that there is ground for my terrible fear in this accursed place! I looked out over the beautiful expanse, bathed in soft yellow moonlight till it was almost as light as day. In the soft light the distant hills became melted, and the shadows in the valleys and gorges of velvety blackness. The mere beauty seemed to cheer me. There was peace and comfort in every breath I drew. As I leaned from the window my eye was caught by something moving a storey below me, and somewhat to my left, where I imagined, from the order of the rooms, that the windows of the Count's own room would look out. The window at which I stood was tall and deep, stone-mullioned, and though weatherworn, was still complete. But it was evidently many a day since the case had been there. I drew back behind the stonework, and looked carefully out.

What I saw was the Count's head coming out from the window. I did not see the face, but I knew the man by the neck and the movement of his back and arms. In any case I could not mistake the hands which I had had some many opportunities of studying. I was at first interested and somewhat amused, for it is wonderful how small a matter will interest and amuse a man when he is a prisoner. But my very feelings changed to repulsion and terror when I saw the whole man slowly emerge from the window and begin to crawl down the castle wall over the dreadful abyss, face down with his cloak spreading out around him like great wings.

At first I could not believe my eyes. I thought it was some trick of the moonlight, some weird effect of shadow, but I kept looking, and it could be no delusion. I saw the fingers and toes grasp the corners of the stones, worn clear of the mortar by the stress of years, and by thus using every projection and inequality move downwards with considerable speed, just as a lizard moves along a wall.

3 The writer at work: structure

> **Examiner tip**
>
> Exam extracts are always introduced with some explanatory text. Make sure you read this to pick up hints about the story and the background to the extract.

> **English term**
>
> *****Narrative:** A spoken or written account; a story

Activity 8

1. Read the extract from *Dracula* and the introductory text twice. Understand what is happening in each paragraph.

   a. Summarise the situation of the narrator, Jonathan Harker, together with his thoughts and feelings. Use no more than 20 words to do this.

   b. Share your summaries with a partner and check that you share a common understanding of the narrative* of the text.

2. Consider how time is used to structure the narrative.

   a. Use the labels below to link each paragraph with the relevant time focus. You may want to write on a printout of the extract to label each paragraph. Look at the verbs in the paragraphs to help you establish the tense as past (happened before) or present (happening now).

   > **Past time** – a memory.

   > **Mixture of past time and present time** – memory and present thoughts or experience.

   > **Present time** – present thoughts or experience.

   b. Identify one or two quotations that justify the time label you have chosen for each paragraph.

3. Consider how setting is used to structure the narrative. Add the labels below for any paragraphs where you think setting is an important focus.

   > The view of the courtyard from Harker's room   Outside the castle

   > Main castle area   Harker's room

4. Read the passage again and annotate or note any sentence forms that are used to help the reader imagine the horror of Harker's situation. Look back to the definitions on page 42 to help you. An example is completed below. Use the same format to write about the examples you choose.

   > Stoker uses a variety of sentence structures to convey a sense of horror in this passage. The single-clause sentence 'Be warned!' of Dracula's reported speech creates a sense of danger about the castle…

3.7 Writing about the structure of prose fiction

You have now considered the organisation of the whole text as well as its sentence structures. Writing about structure requires you to:

- establish the overall focus of the text in relation to the question set and the writer's intention
- consider the overall movement across the extract (for example, from wide focus to detail, from outside to inside, from one person or event to another)
- identify structural features using the correct terminology
- locate evidence by using quotation, line reference or paragraph reference
- comment on the effect on the reader and its link to the writer's intention.

Activity 9

Complete the response to the following task – it has been started for you.

> 'Comment on how structure is used by Stoker in this passage to convey Harker's experiences.'

> This passage describes Harker's experience on his arrival at Count Dracula's castle, as recorded in his diary. This format allows Stoker to structure the passage combining the present time as Harker writes his diary and his memories, as he thinks about the strange experiences of this day. The extract begins with a memory – 'he finished his speech' – and the past time is used so that the warnings of Count Dracula add to the reader's understanding of the fear Harker is experiencing about the things that have happened that day.
> NEW PARAGRAPH: The next paragraph moves forward in time...
> NEW PARAGRAPH: Stoker also uses setting to structure this extract, as the focus moves from the shared areas of the castle to Harker in his own room there, writing his diary...
> NEW PARAGRAPH: Stoker uses a variety of sentence structures to convey the strangeness of Harker's experiences and the horror of his situation...

Writing about a sub-extract

You can apply what you have learned about structure to a shorter extract, such as a paragraph or two. To analyse a sub-extract you should ask yourself the following questions.

1	How is the sub-extract built? Are there distinct sections?
2	What is the focus of each distinct section?
3	How do the sub-sections work together? For example is there any contrast, repetition or link between them?
4	Is there a point of change or shift?
5	How is the extract built in terms of sentence structures?

For all these questions consider the writer's reasons for their choices.

3 The writer at work: structure

Activity 10

Now read the second paragraph of the *Dracula* extract again. Consider the few annotations that have been made on the passage and add more of your own to answer questions 1–5 on the previous page.

Single-clause sentence – simple statement to emphasise change of setting and being alone

Past event – memory

Time changes – alternating past and present time – his present feelings are combined to show horror

> When he left me I went to my room. After a little while, not hearing any sound, I came out and went up the stone stair to where I could look out towards the South. There was some sense of freedom in the vast expanse, inaccessible though it was to me, as compared with the narrow darkness of the courtyard. Looking out on this, I felt that I was indeed in prison, and I seemed to want a breath of fresh air, though it were of the night. I am beginning to feel this nocturnal existence tell on me. It is destroying my nerve. I start at my own shadow, and am full of all sorts of horrible imaginings. God knows that there is ground for my terrible fear in this accursed place! I looked out over the beautiful expanse, bathed in soft yellow moonlight till it was almost as light as day. In the soft light the distant hills became melted, and the shadows in the valleys and gorges of velvety blackness. The mere beauty seemed to cheer me. There was peace and comfort in every breath I drew. As I leaned from the window my eye was caught by something moving a storey below me, and somewhat to my left, where I imagined, from the order of the rooms, that the windows of the Count's own room would look out. The window at which I stood was tall and deep, stone-mullioned, and though weatherworn, was still complete. But it was evidently many a day since the case had been there. I drew back behind the stonework, and looked carefully out.

Change of setting – a change from being in the whole castle to being on his own in his room and nearby areas

Activity 11

Read the question and student response below. The student has made various clear points. However, there is not enough evidence or reference to the text. There is little link to the focus of the question about the writer's intention.

> 'Analyse how the writer uses structure to reflect changes in the narrator's mood.'

> In this passage the writer uses structure to reflect the narrator's mood changing from curiosity about the building he is in, to becoming more cheerful and then finally some sense of curiosity and concern.

46

3.7 Writing about the structure of prose fiction

1. Identify the words in this response that show the candidate is keeping a focus on 'mood' as set by the question.

   The opening of the extract marks a change of setting as the narrator returns to being on his own in his room. He leaves this safety and begins to explore the areas of his room, moving upwards in the castle. At this early point in the paragraph, he feels relaxed and more free which marks a shift in his mood from rather depressed to more content. There is a contrast in the two settings described, between the dark inner building of the castle and the bright natural world of the view from the window. However, another shift in the final section of the paragraph is marked as he 'leaned from the window' and his mood changes to curiosity and maybe concern at this point.

2. Which of the following does the candidate use to create an effective analysis of structure? Support your answer by finding evidence from the response.

   subject-specific terminology   quotations   references to locations in the text

3. Improve the answer by adding two points about how sentence structures convey the narrator's mood. Remember to use subject-specific terminology supported by quotations or textual references.

47

Mini Assessment

Assessment objective

- Explain, comment on and analyse how writers use structure to achieve effects and influence readers, using relevant subject terminology to support their views (AO2)

Mini Assessment 1: prose fiction

The skills you have secured in this section focus on analysing and commenting on how writers use structure to achieve effects and influence readers.

The assessment below will allow you to test your skills and review your progress in this area in preparation for exam-focused work.

Read through the final three paragraphs of the extract from *Dracula* on page 43, from 'When he left me' to the end. Then complete the following activities.

1. Identify the point where the writer changes from past to present time. How do the narrator's past experiences affect his present mood?

2. Identify the line that reflects a turning point in the narrator's mood.

3. Identify an example of the writer 'zooming in' to a particular detail.

4. Use your answers to write a more detailed answer to the question:

   'How does the writer use structure to reflect the narrator's mood?'

Mini Assessment 2: non-fiction

'The Walk' by Rebecca Hawkes

Read this newspaper article introducing a new film *The Walk*. It focuses on the famous high wire walker, Philippe Petit.

The Walk — trailer: first look at Joseph Gordon Levitt as 'man on wire' Philippe Petit

Joseph Gordon-Levitt stars in Robert Zemeckis' forthcoming film about Philippe Petit, the man who walked between the Twin Towers of the World Trade Center

By Rebecca Hawkes   2:55PM GMT 09 Dec 2014

On August 7, 1974, a man named Philippe Petit stepped out on to a high wire, suspended between the Twin Towers of New York's World Trade Center, 1350 feet above the ground. He performed there for 45 minutes, making a total of eight passes along the wire.

The stunt — which was carried out with no official permission, and no safety net — took years of planning.

Man On Wire, a critically acclaimed documentary about Petit, was released in 2008. Now, Forrest Gump director Robert Zemeckis has turned Petit's story into a feature film, starring Joseph Gordon-Levitt as the high wire artist.

Using the latest in state-of-the-art visual effects, 3D and IMAX technology, as well as a massive set construction, Zemeckis and Gordon-Levitt have recreated Petit's historical walk. The vertigo-inducing trailer for the film, released

Mini Assessment

today on the *Telegraph*'s website, depicts Gordon-Levitt as Petit, standing on top of the World Trade Center, testing the balance of a metal beam.

Given the tragic history of the Twin Towers, it's understandable that many people will feel strange seeing them recreated on film. But Gordon-Levitt and Zemeckis see The Walk as a tribute to the skyscrapers.

'The movie is a love letter to the Twin Towers,' says Zemeckis, in a press release. 'They're very much present in the film as characters. So it's also a celebration. In the tragic history of those buildings, this is one glorious and human moment that happened. I think that's something that's important to remember too.'

The Walk also stars Ben Kingsley, Charlotte Le Bon, James Badge Dale and Ben Schwartz, and will be released in October 2015.

1. Name two of the structural features that are used to begin this article.
2. Give a subtitle to each paragraph to identify the main topic. For example, the main topic of the first paragraph could be titled, 'The facts of the event'.
3. Comment on three examples of sentence forms used by the writer and how they contribute to the way the article conveys information.
4. Identify the line that reflects a turning point as the article shifts from historical information to the present time.
5. Use your answers to write a more detailed answer to the question:

   'How does the writer use structure to convey information about the new film and its background?'

Examiner tip
Remember to look at any titles/headlines, subtitles or sub-headings given by the writer to help you understand a non-fiction extract.

Self-assessment
Look back at the work you have done in this chapter. You can now review your performance of the skills you have practised.

The skills of reading AO2 Structure are specifically tested in question 3 Paper 1 Fiction and Imaginative Writing and question 3 Paper 2 Non-fiction and Transactional Writing.

Skill	🟢 🟠 🔴
I can understand how a text is structured.	
I can identify structural features.	
I can use relevant subject terminology to comment on structure.	
I can explain how writers use structure to achieve effects.	
I can analyse how structure is used to influence the reader.	

4 Focusing on language and structure

Reading

Assessment objective

- Explain, comment on and analyse how writers use language and structure to achieve effects and influence readers, using relevant subject terminology to support their views (AO2)

Assessment links

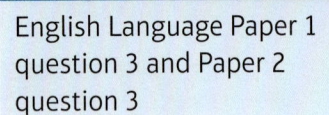

English Language Paper 1 question 3 and Paper 2 question 3

Texts

The extracts for analysis in this unit should be downloaded and printed from the Active Teach Library (see page v) so that they can be read in full and annotated.

4.1 Text at sentence and word level

In Units 2 and 3, you learned about both language and structural features. It is useful to be able to distinguish these two aspects of a written text. However, they do not work to achieve the writer's aims in isolation. The writer builds the whole text, by planning the complete construction, considering sentence forms and making choices about individual phrases and devices at word level. These aspects work together to achieve the writer's overall intentions.

Activity 1

1. Discuss the terms listed below with a partner to check you know the meaning of each one.

Rhetorical question | Quotation | List | Punctuation types (e.g. ellipsis; question mark; colon) | Sentence types (e.g. long, short, single clause, multi-clause)

Dialogue | Shifts in time/place/character/mood/atmosphere/attitudes/ideas | Headline | Language devices (e.g. alliteration, onomatopoeia) | Specialist terminology

Title | Heading | Paragraph | Introduction | Conclusion | Salutation and closing | Caption | Beginning

Examiner tip

Remind yourself of the aspects of language and structure learned so far. Refer back to Unit 3.

2. Add the above items to the table below to indicate whether each one is a structural or language feature.

Structure (whole text and sentence level)	Language (word level)
Prediction/foreshadowing Repetition or contrast (of ideas or phrases across a text) Lead Subtitle Section	Parts of speech (e.g. noun, verb, adverb, adjective, pronoun) Repetition of word/words in close proximity Figurative language (e.g. imagery, symbolism)

Extract from *My philosophy of boxing* by Muhammad Ali

In the exam you will be asked to write about language and structure. Read the opening of a short essay by the boxer Muhammad Ali on the next page. The annotations mark language and structural features used to convey Ali's personal approach to boxing.

4.1 Text at sentence and word level

My philosophy of boxing by Muhammad Ali — **Title** – establishes an essay of ideas

I always believed boxers should not hurt each other unnecessarily just to please the crowd.

Opening – single sentence paragraph – introduces key message

Most fighters are scared to lighten up during a bout even when winning on points, for fear they will be accused of being part of a fixed fight. I can remember watching other fighters and thinking, 'Boy, I must be a fool. These two men are like two roosters at a cockfight whose owners have strapped knives to their spurs and had them fight each other to satisfy the crowds who bet on them.'

Specialist boxing terminology – reflects his knowledge of the sport

Contrast – he is different from others

Simple sentence – emphasises his difference

Simile – men like animals not humans

Activity 2

Now read the next four paragraphs and annotate them yourself, in the same way. You should work on a printout of the text. Identify each method (language or structure) and add a note about its effect. One example is done for you. You can use the terms below to support your work, or use your own ideas.

Compound sentence – mutual benefits

I love boxing and it did a lot for me. But sometimes it made me think about how savage human beings could be to each other. That wasn't the kind of boxer I wanted to be. My strategy was to be as scientific as I could when I fought. I didn't want to be seriously hurt, and I didn't want to do that to anybody else either.

My plan was to dance, stay out of my opponents reach, and use my wits as much as my fists. I tried to get into the mind of my opponent and psyche him out. I studied my opponents to learn their strengths and weaknesses and to the best of my ability I tried to be completely honest about my own. That was pretty much how I won the championship fight with Sonny Liston, and how I won the title back in my match with George Foreman.

Muslims aren't supposed to trick people, and I try not to do that. I love magic, and at one time I was a member of a magicians' union. But because Muslims aren't supposed to deceive anyone, I would always reveal how a trick was done after I amazed everyone with my 'magic powers'. After I did this on a British television show, however, the magicians' union kicked me out.

Just as when doing magic tricks, boxing requires practice and dedication. Showmanship is a large part of both boxing and magic as well. I called my opponents names and boasted of my abilities and beauty, and often predicted the round of my victory to infuriate them so they would make mistakes. Some may call this a trick, I just hoped it gave me the edge.

| First person pronoun – emphasises personal beliefs | Short simple sentence – confident in his belief | Following paragraph – details his strategy | Compound sentence – balance |

Verbs of action… | Informal language… | Anecdote… | Proper nouns…

Mini Assessment

Assessment objective

- Explain, comment on and analyse how writers use language and structure to achieve effects and influence readers, using relevant subject terminology to support their views (AO2)

Glossary

***The old guard:** Old-fashioned people

***Congolese:** People from the Republic of Congo, the Democratic Republic of the Congo, or the area surrounding the Congo River

The skills you have secured in this section focus on analysing and commenting on how writers use structure to achieve effects and influence readers.

The assessment below will allow you to test your skills and review your progress in this area in preparation for exam-focused work. The skills are directly transferable to fiction texts.

Extract from 'Obituary: Muhammad Ali'

Read through the opening of an obituary of Muhammad Ali taken from *The Economist*. After years of suffering from Parkinson's disease, Ali, one of the world's greatest sporting figures, died in 2016. An obituary is a public article written after the death of a person, giving facts about their life and celebrating their achievements.

The greatest

Obituary: Muhammad Ali

Muhammad Ali, heavyweight boxer, died on June 3rd, aged 74

PURE skill was much of it. The brutal delicacy of the ring-craft, so rare in the heavyweight division. Among the lumbering sloggers he dodged and danced, floating like a butterfly, stinging like a bee. Faced with a solid, flat-footed opponent, as all seemed to be compared with him, he would circle, torment and mesmerise, throwing short punches at speed. All that weaving, skipping, leaning leisurely away, before coming in for the kill. Flooring Sonny Liston once with a punch so fast that no one quite saw it (see above). Taunting George Foreman to exhaustion by sinking into the slack ropes, just letting him punch himself out while his own fine, hard body absorbed the blows. He always knew when his rivals would topple. He would mimic their shuffling desperation and his own artistry, pummelling the air with fast, precise, furious fists. Let the old guard* complain that he ducked and dipped too much, held his hands too low and his chin cocked too high; he won fights.

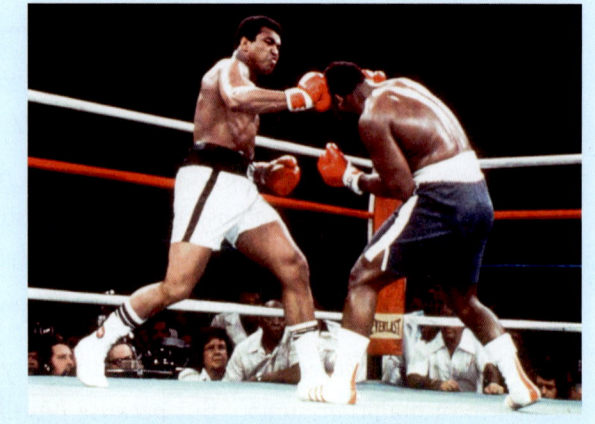

And what fights. Fifty-six of them in his career, and only five defeats. One against Liston in 1964, when he was 22 and the odds were 7–1 against him, that left the world heavyweight champion too beat up after six rounds to come out of his corner. One against Cleveland Williams that was watched by the biggest indoor crowd yet seen in boxing, 35,460 people. The Rumble in the Jungle in Kinshasa in 1974, at which 60,000 Congolese* cried 'Ali, boumayé! Ali, kill him!' The Thrilla in Manila against Joe Frazier the next year, fought in 100-degree heat, to retain his title when he was 33 years old. Boxing had never been so entertaining or so global. In the whole bruised and bloody history of the sport, there had never been such a star.

Mini Assessment

1. Identify the TAPS (Text type, Audience, Purpose, Source) of this non-fiction article.

2. Consider the following structural elements in relation to these paragraphs. Select three that you think are the most important and select the best quotation or textual reference to illustrate each one:

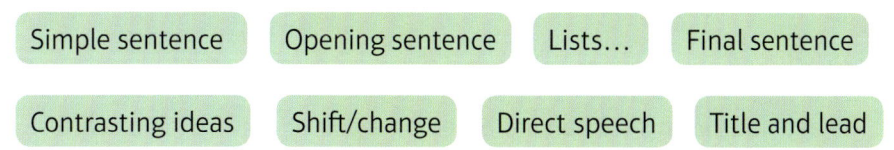

   Simple sentence   Opening sentence   Lists…   Final sentence

   Contrasting ideas   Shift/change   Direct speech   Title and lead

3. Using your work from task 2 above, write a paragraph to analyse how structure is used to celebrate Ali's life. Use textual references to support your points.

4. Consider the following language elements in relation to the extract. Select three that you think are the most important and select the best quotation to illustrate each one:

   Simile   Verbs of action   Proper nouns

   Adjectives to describe   Rhyme   Facts and statistics

5. Write a paragraph to analyse how language is used to celebrate Ali's life. Use textual references to support your points.

> **Examiner tip**
>
> See Unit 6 page 77 for further explanation of TAPS.

> **Examiner tip**
>
> Remember that you cannot always quote a structural feature; you may need to use a line reference or paragraph reference to locate your example.

Self-assessment

Look back at the work you have done in this unit. You can now review your performance on the skills you have practised.

The skills of reading AO2 Structure are specifically tested in Paper 1 question 3 and Paper 2 question 3.

Skill	🟢 🟠 🔴
I can identify language and structural features.	
I can use relevant subject terminology to comment on language and structure.	
I can select detailed and appropriate references to fully support my points.	
I can explore how language and structure are used to achieve effects and influence readers.	

5 Synthesising and comparing

Reading

Assessment objectives

- Select and synthesise evidence from different texts (AO1)
- Compare writers' ideas and perspectives, as well as how these are conveyed, across two or more texts (AO3)

Assessment links

English Language Paper 2 Questions 7a and 7b

English term

***Synthesis:** Bringing together related elements, information or ideas in two or more texts

Texts

The extracts for analysis in this unit should be downloaded and printed from the Active Teach Library (see page v) so that they can be read in full and annotated.

5.1 Synthesising two texts

The activities in this section are based on a pair of non-fiction extracts: *A Parrot in the Pepper Tree* by Chris Stewart and *The Home of the Blizzard* by Sir Douglas Mawson.

To make an effective synthesis*, you need to pull together the key similarities in the two extracts which are addressed in the question. Try to link similar ideas and information. You also need to find evidence from both texts to support the similarities you find.

Activity 1

Read the entries in the table below, which shows information about what is described in two non-fiction texts.

Text A	Text B
worried about car breaking down	snow is falling and the wind is strong
feels the journey is long and miserable	companion becoming miserable
the temperature is minus 25 degrees	covering long distances on foot

Write down which of the points above are **similar** in some way.

Activity 2

Look closely at the two extracts.

Text A: *A Parrot in the Pepper Tree*

It was late at night and for six long hours I had been driving along an icy tunnel of road into the snowy forest of northern Sweden. I hunched stiffly over the steering wheel to peer along a dismal beam at the monotony of pine trees and snow. One of my headlights had already given up the ghost, snuffed out in a futile struggle against the lashing ice and minus twenty-five degrees cold, and beyond the feeble pallor of its mate and the dim green glow of my dashboard there spread an endless blackness.

5.1 Synthesising two texts

Text B: *The Home of the Blizzard*

By 9am we had accomplished a splendid march of fifteen miles three hundred and fifty yards, but the satisfaction we should have felt at making such an inroad on the huge task before us was damped by the fact that I suddenly became aware that Mertz was not as cheerful as usual. I was at a loss to know the reason, for he was always such a bright and companionable fellow.

Explain a point of similarity between these two texts for each of the following aspects:

- situations
- problems
- moods.

Use short quotations from the texts to support the points you make.

Activity 3

Now look at two more short extracts from the same texts.

Text A: *A Parrot in the Pepper Tree*

For more than an hour, now, not a single car had passed me, and not a single lamplight glimmered through the trees. Country Swedes have an appealing tradition of leaving a light burning all night in the window to cheer the passing traveller, but for miles there had been nothing but the deep black of the star-studded sky, and the withering cold. Cocooned in the fuggy warmth of my hired Volvo I had the feeling of being further away from my fellow man than I had ever thought possible.

Text B: *The Home of the Blizzard*

The light was so atrocious for marching that, after stumbling along for two and a half miles, we were obliged to give up the attempt and camp, spending the day in sleeping-bags.

In the evening at 9.30pm the sun appeared for a brief moment and the wind subsided. Another stage was therefore attempted but at considerable cost, for we staggered along in the bewildering light, continually falling over unseen sastrugi*.

1. Read the following example of a synthesis of the two texts.

   Both texts describe trying to get away from the outside world to be cosy. Text A mentions being in the 'hired Volvo' and B mentions 'spending the day in sleeping bags'.

2. Write a paragraph adding a new point of synthesis to the student answer above.

Glossary

*****Sastrugi:** Ridges or grooves formed by the wind on the surface of hard snow

5 Synthesising and comparing

> **Examiner tip**
>
> Remember that synthesis is just asking you to find similarities with evidence. You do not need to analyse language or comment on how the writer has achieved effects.

> **Examiner tip**
>
> When you first compare two texts, focus on what they have in common. You can then begin to think about the ways in which they differ.

5.2 Making a comparison

Comparing purpose and content

The activities in this section are based on a new pairing of texts, 'Puppy love: "Do I like dogs more than people?"' by Will Storr and *In the Shadow of Man* by Jane Goodall.

Text C: 'Puppy love: "Do I like dogs more than people?"'

> More than her behaviour, what began to astonish me was the constant to-ing and fro-ing of communication. When she walked into a room, I'd say, 'Hello' and she'd respond with four cheery wags of her tail. When I left scraps on my plate, she'd look at me, then at the plate, then, very slowly, back at me again. [...] On the occasions we'd row, she'd paw at the aggressor, licking their face and wagging her tail until it was impossible to argue any more for giggling.

Text D: *In the Shadow of Man*

> As I watched, still scarcely believing it was true, I saw two more chimpanzee heads peering at me over the grass from the other side of a small forest glade: a female and a youngster. They bobbed down as I turned my head toward them, but soon reappeared, one after the other, in the lower branches of a tree about forty yards away. There they sat, almost motionless, watching me.
>
> For over half a year I had been trying to overcome the chimpanzees' inherent fear of me, the fear that made them vanish into the undergrowth whenever I approached. At first they had fled even when I was as far away as five hundred yards and on the other side of a ravine. Now two males were sitting so close that I could almost hear them breathing.

Activity 4

You need to focus on the purpose* and content of the two texts.

1. As you read, note down **who**, **what** and **where** the text is about under these headings.

   People   Places   Events

2. Which of these purposes does each text have?

   describe   explain   persuade   inform

   argue   advise   entertain

> **English term**
>
> *****Purpose:** The overall aim of a text

56

5.2 Making a comparison

3. Look at the notes you have made in tasks 1 and 2. What similarities and differences can you identify in **Text C** and **Text D**? Write one or two sentences summarising your ideas. You could use some of the words and phrases below to help you.

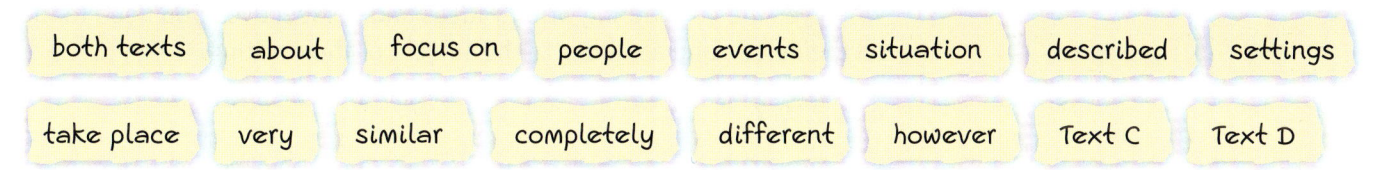

   both texts · about · focus on · people · events · situation · described · settings

   take place · very · similar · completely · different · however · Text C · Text D

Activity 5

Think about any similarities or differences in the writers' perspectives in **Text C** and **Text D**.

1. Are the texts written in the first person*, describing their personal experiences, thoughts and feelings? Or are they written in the third person*, giving information about the experiences of other people?

2. How would you describe the writers' attitudes to their experiences? You could use some of the ideas below, or your own ideas.

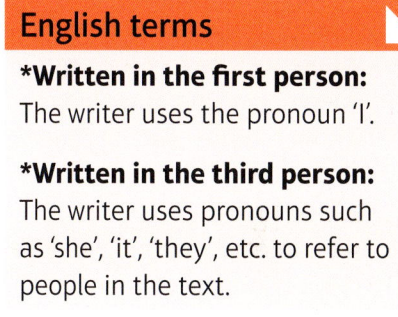

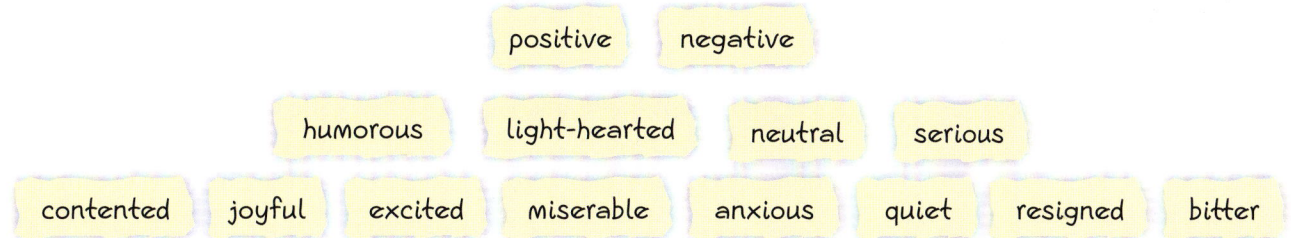

> **English terms**
>
> ***Written in the first person:**
> The writer uses the pronoun 'I'.
>
> ***Written in the third person:**
> The writer uses pronouns such as 'she', 'it', 'they', etc. to refer to people in the text.

positive · negative

humorous · light-hearted · neutral · serious

contented · joyful · excited · miserable · anxious · quiet · resigned · bitter

Activity 6

You are now going to compare the writers' ideas and perspectives.

1. Note down what you can infer from **Text C** about the writers' ideas and perspectives about his new puppy. Give evidence from the text.

2. Note down what you can infer from **Text D** about the writers' ideas and perspectives about the chimpanzees. Remember to use textual evidence.

3. Compare the **ideas and perspectives** about animals in the two texts. Write a sentence or two summarising them, using quotations from the text. You could use some of the adverbial phrases below to signal whether you are highlighting a similarity or a difference.

   in the same way · similarly · however · on the other hand

57

5 Synthesising and comparing

5.3 Identifying ideas and perspectives

Writers express their perspectives through their focus on ideas and information, and through the language and structural choices they make.

When you are considering writers' ideas and perspectives, you need to focus on their views and attitudes to the subject of their writing.

Activity 7

Read **Text C** again, in which the writer describes the experience of getting a new dog.

1. Now look at some key quotations from **Text C**.

A When my wife told me she wanted a dog, I briefly imagined a kind of walking ornament that would lie at my feet in the evenings and come with me to the shops.

B It was November and I spent countless freezing hours begging it to go to the toilet in the garden instead of on the rugs.

C After another morning spent shampooing muck, I'd had enough. Parker was a bad idea. 'She's broken. I don't think we can keep her.'

D More than her behaviour, what began to astonish me was the constant to-ing and fro-ing of communication.

E And by this point, I couldn't believe how much I loved her.

F There's no doubt that Parker has silently, mysteriously, conquered our household.

G She joins us in bed and there we snore, three happy heads on the pillows.

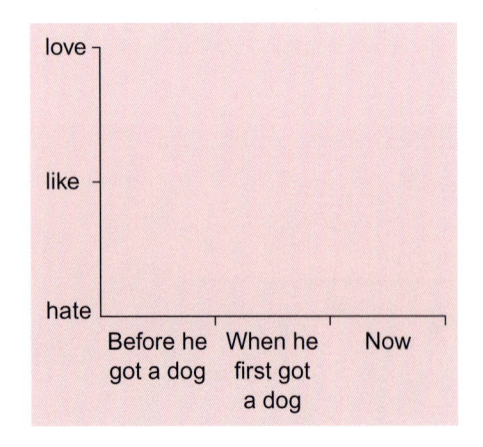

2. Copy and complete the graph on the left, tracking the writer's views and attitudes to his dog. You should mark a cross on the graph and label each one with the letter of the quotation.

3. Which of the key quotations above **clearly** and **explicitly** state the writer's views and attitudes to his dog? Note down the letter of each one.

4. Which of the key quotations above **suggest** or **imply** the writer's views and attitudes to his dog? Note down the letter of each one.

5. Choose three of the key quotations that show how the writer's views and attitudes to his dog change. Identify at least one word or phrase in each that reveals his views and attitudes.

6. Write three or four sentences summing up the writer's changing ideas and perspectives on his new dog. Support your ideas with quotations from the text.

5.3 Identifying ideas and perspectives

Activity 8

Look closely at these two extracts from **Text C** and **Text D**:

Text C: 'Puppy love: "Do I like dogs more than people?"'

Within 48 hours, it arrived, an eight-week labradoodle, carried in Farrah's arms over the threshold. [...] It was called Parker. 'It's cute,' I said, extending a finger in welcome, which it bit.

It immediately became apparent that the fact of my working at home meant the raising of this baby animal would fall to me. It was November and I spent countless freezing hours begging it to go to the toilet in the garden instead of on the rugs. I was hardly getting any work done. And the cost!

Text D: *In the Shadow of Man*

The distance between us was too great for me to make detailed observations, so I decided to try to get closer. I surveyed the trees close to the group: if I could manage to get to that large fig without frightening the chimpanzees, I thought, I would get an excellent view. It took me about ten minutes to make the journey. As I moved cautiously around the thick gnarled trunk of the fig I realised that the chimpanzees had gone; the branches of the fruit tree were empty. The same old feeling of depression clawed at me. Once again the chimpanzees had seen me and silently fled. Then all at once my heart missed several beats.

Write a paragraph comparing the writers' ideas and perspectives on animals in these two extracts. In your paragraph you could:

- State the difference between the writer of **Text C**'s views and attitudes to his dog, and the writer of **Text D**'s views and attitudes to chimpanzees.
- Identify a relevant quotation from **Text C** and explain how it shows the writer's attitude.
- Identify a relevant quotation from **Text D** and explain how it shows the writer's attitude.

5 Synthesising and comparing

5.4 Selecting evidence

The following activities relate to the texts *A Parrot in the Pepper Tree* and *The Home of the Blizzard*.

The most effective evidence shows the writer's ideas and perspectives and allows you to explore how they use language and structure to convey them.

Activity 9

Read **Text A: *A Parrot in the Pepper Tree***, in which the writer describes a journey through Sweden at night. Now look at some sentences from the first paragraph of **Text A**.

A I hunched stiffly over the steering wheel to peer along a dismal beam at the monotony of pine trees and snow.

B One of my headlights had already given up the ghost, snuffed out in a futile struggle against the lashing ice and minus twenty-five degrees cold, and beyond the feeble pallor of its mate and the dim green glow of my dashboard there spread an endless blackness.

C For more than an hour, now, not a single car had passed me, and not a single lamplight glimmered through the trees.

D Cocooned in the fuggy warmth of my hired Volvo I had the feeling of being further away from my fellow man than I had ever thought possible.

> **Examiner tip**
> Notice whether the writer uses first person 'I' or third person 'she' to convey their views.

1. Note down the letters (A, B, etc.) of the sentences in which the writer conveys his ideas and perspectives on his journey.

2. Look again at sentence A. Which **words or phrases** in this sentence convey the writer's ideas and perspectives? Use them as evidence to complete the sentence below.

   > The writer creates the impression of a long, boring, miserable journey, using the words …

> **Examiner tip**
> Remember, you don't need to use the whole sentence as evidence – just the relevant parts that show how the writer has structured it.

3. Look again at sentence C. How does the writer use sentence structure to emphasise his feelings of loneliness? Complete the sentence below using evidence from sentence C.

   > The writer emphasises his feelings of isolation and loneliness by…

4. Look at sentences B and D. Which one contains the more effective evidence supporting the writer's ideas and perspectives? To help you make your choice, ask yourself:
   - Does this sentence reveal the writer's ideas and perspectives?
   - Does the writer's language choice reveal his ideas and perspectives?
   - Does the writer's choice of sentence structure help to convey his ideas and perspectives?

   Write one or two sentences explaining your choice.

5.4 Selecting evidence

Activity 10

Look at these short extracts from Text A and Text B.

Text A: *A Parrot in the Pepper Tree*

The radio was little help. The only station I had managed to pick up seemed entirely devoted to accordion and fiddle dances, the sort of low-key jolly fare you might expect at the funeral of a popular dog. I found it a little depressing. Instead, to keep awake, I fell into practising Mandarin Chinese, which for years I had been trying to learn. Counting out loud to yourself, *yi, er, san, si, wu*, is a good way of getting the hang of the tones and it helped me to forget how incredibly lonely I felt. Every time I got to a hundred or so, I would allow my mind to skip back to my home in Spain — the sun on a terrace of orange and lemon trees, Ana, my wife, and I lying on the grass, squinting up through the leaves, while our daughter Chloë hurled sticks for the dog — and then homesickness would strike with an almost physical stab and I'd start again — *yi, er, san, si, wu…*

Text B: *The Home of the Blizzard*

The light was so atrocious for marching that, after stumbling along for two and a half miles, we were obliged to give up the attempt and camp, spending the day in sleeping-bags.

In the evening at 9.30pm the sun appeared for a brief moment and the wind subsided. Another stage was therefore attempted but at considerable cost, for we staggered along in the bewildering light, continually falling over unseen sastrugi.

1. Compare the writers' ideas and perspectives on their journey in the extracts from Text A and Text B above. Are they similar or different?
2. Write a paragraph explaining how they are similar or different. Aim to:
   - select evidence that clearly shows each writer's ideas and perspectives
   - comment on each writer's use of language and/or sentence structure.

5 Synthesising and comparing

5.5 Comparing writers' methods

The following activities relate to the texts 'Puppy love: "Do I like dogs more than people?"' and *In the Shadow of Man*.

When you compare the writers' ideas and perspectives in two texts, you also need to compare the ways in which they convey them. This could be a comparison of the language choices they use to convey similar ideas, or different ways in which they highlight or emphasise their perspectives. You should pay attention to words, phrases and sentences.

Activity 11

Read both of the extracts below. Each writer clearly states their thoughts and feelings about animals – but they also reveal their ideas and perspectives through their descriptions of the animals' appearance and behaviour.

Text C: 'Puppy love: "Do I like dogs more than people?"'

> Then there were her own peculiar wants: her love for Mini Babybels, swimming, BBC nature documentaries and cartoonishly huge sticks. She'd made the odd decision that her bedtime was 22:30. Every night at that point, give or take 10 minutes, she'd give a noisy yawn and trot happily upstairs. The continual, daily surprise was that Parker was a creature of her own wills, moods and curiosities. And by this point, I couldn't believe how much I loved her.

Text D: *In the Shadow of Man*

> Without any doubt whatsoever, this was the proudest moment I had known. I had been accepted by the two magnificent creatures grooming each other in front of me. I knew them both – David Graybeard, who had always been the least afraid of me, was one and the other was Goliath, not the giant his name implies but of superb physique and the highest-ranking of all the males. Their coats gleamed vivid black in the softening light of the evening.

1. Copy and complete the table below, adding **at least two** quotations from each text in which the writers create an impression of the animals they are describing.

Text C: Puppy love	Text D: In the Shadow of Man
'her love for Mini Babybels, swimming, BBC nature documentaries and cartoonishly huge sticks'	'magnificent creatures'

5.5 Comparing writers' methods

2. Look at the quotations you have noted. Copy and complete the table below, ticking either '**Text C**' or '**Text D**' to compare the ways in which the writers describe the animals' appearance and behaviour.

	Text C ✓	Text D ✓
Focuses on appearance		
Focuses on behaviour		
Suggests admiration		
Suggests affection		
Uses adjectives		
Uses a list		
Creates humour		
Creates a vivid image		

Activity 12

How do the writers' choices in each text, and the impressions they create, reveal their ideas and perspectives on the animals they are writing about?

1. Write a response explaining your ideas, using the quotations and notes you have gathered from this page and the opposite page. You could use the sentence fragments below.

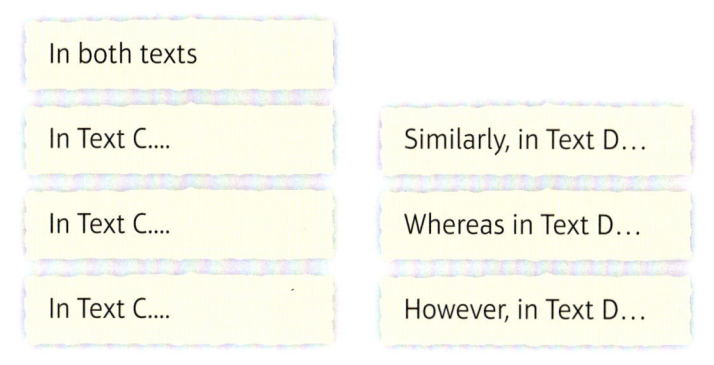

   In both texts

   In Text C....   Similarly, in Text D…

   In Text C....   Whereas in Text D…

   In Text C....   However, in Text D…

2. When you have written your paragraph, check that you have:
   - compared the writers' ideas and perspectives
   - used quotations from both texts
   - commented on ways in which the writers' choices in both texts reveal their ideas and perspectives.

5 Synthesising and comparing

5.6 Structuring a comparison

The following activities relate to the texts 'Puppy love: "Do I like dogs more than people?"' and *In the Shadow of Man*.

In your comparison, you need to identify each writer's ideas and perspectives and explore how the writers' choices convey those ideas and perspectives in key quotations from both texts.

Sequencing your ideas

When you have noted the different ideas and perspectives you are going to compare in your response, you need to sequence them in a logical order. It is often useful to begin your answer with a broad, general point of similarity or difference.

Activity 13

Look at this broad point of similarity.

> Both writers emphasise the hard work, determination and effort they give to the animals they are writing about.

1. Find a quotation from **Text C** and a quotation from **Text D** to support this point.

2. Explain how the writers' choices in these quotations convey their ideas and perspectives.

3. Use the quotations and ideas you have noted to write a paragraph beginning with the broad point of comparison above. You could use some of the words and phrases below to link your ideas.

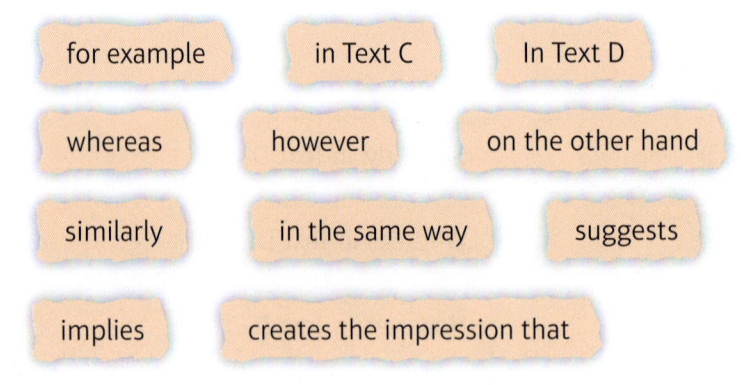

for example	in Text C	In Text D
whereas	however	on the other hand
similarly	in the same way	suggests
implies	creates the impression that	

5.6 Structuring a comparison

Activity 14

Look at this student's paragraph, comparing **Text C** and **Text D**:

> Both writers really like the animals they write about. The writer of Text C likes his dog because he says 'I couldn't believe how much I loved her'. The writer of Text D likes chimpanzees because she says 'Without any doubt whatsoever, this was the proudest moment I had known.' Both these quotes show how much the writers like the animals they write about.

Think about some of the ways in which this student could improve their paragraph.

1. How could the student develop their comments on the writers' choices in each quotation? Note down your ideas, focusing on the ways in which the writers' choices convey how much they like the animals they write about.

2. What other evidence could the student have added to this paragraph to support the key point it makes? Note down at least one further quotation from each text.

3. Now think about how the writers' choices in each of the quotations you have chosen convey their ideas and perspectives. Note your ideas.

4. Look carefully at the vocabulary the student has used to express their ideas in the paragraph above. Could their ideas and analysis be expressed more precisely? Note your ideas.

5. Use all the ideas you have noted to re-write, improve and develop the ideas and analysis in the student's response above.

Mini Assessment

Assessment objective
- Select and synthesise evidence from different texts (AO1)
- Compare writers' ideas and perspectives, as well as how these are conveyed, across two or more texts (AO3)

The skills you have developed in this unit focus on selecting and sythethising evidence from different texts, and comparing writers' ideas and perspectives.

The assessment on these two pages will allow you to test your skills of comparison and review your progress in preparation for exam-focused work.

Compare two texts

1. Read the full texts of *A Parrot in the Pepper Tree* and *The Home of the Blizzard*. Complete two tables like the ones below, adding as many rows as you need. List all the similar and different views and perspectives that you can find, supported with evidence from the texts.

Similarity	Text A evidence	Text B evidence

Difference	Text A evidence	Text B evidence

2. Select and note down **three key points of comparison** between the ideas and perspectives you have identified in **Text A** and the ideas and perspectives you have identified in **Text B**. These are the key points you will focus on in your comparison.

3. Highlight words, phrases or sentences that convey the writers' ideas and perspectives on their journeys.

Mini Assessment

Write and review

4. Write your comparison of the writers' ideas and perspectives on their journeys in **Text A** and **Text B**.

5. Review your comparison. Have you:

   - supported each of your ideas with evidence from both texts
   - commented on the ways in which the writers' choices convey their ideas and perspectives on their journeys
   - expressed your ideas clearly and precisely?

   Look closely at any of the bullet points you have not achieved. Review, revise and improve your comparison if necessary.

Self-assessment

Look back at the work you have done in this unit. You can now review your performance on the skills you have practised.

The skills of synthesis (AO1) and comparison (AO3) are tested in Paper 2 Questions 7a and 7b.

Skill	🟢 🟠 🔴
I can synthesise information from two texts.	
I can identify the writers' ideas and perspectives.	
I can compare the writers' ideas and perspectives in two texts.	
I can comment on, and compare, how the writers' choices convey their ideas and perspectives in two texts.	
I can structure an effective comparison.	

6 Evaluation

Reading

Assessment objective
- Evaluate texts critically and support this with appropriate textual references (AO4)

Assessment links
English Language Paper 1 question 4 and Paper 2 question 6

Texts
The extracts for analysis in this unit should be downloaded and printed from the Active Teach Library (see page v) so that they can be read in full and annotated.

6.1 The meaning of 'evaluation'

Evaluation means:

Stand back to look at the whole → Consider its overall impact in relation to the 'big idea' behind it → Make a judgement about the creator's success

Examiner tip

Evaluation of a text requires you to look at the whole 'from a distance'.

Analysis of language and structure requires you to look carefully at the smaller details.

To understand how to evaluate a text you can think about the architecture of a very different building. The Al Wakrah FIFA Stadium in Qatar was designed to convey a 'big idea' about its country's world reputation for the 2022 World Cup.

Activity 1

Consider how the design of the Al Wakrah Stadium conveys ideas about this small but powerful Arab desert state. Look at the image below. You might like to watch a short film of the Al Wakrah Stadium (available online) to inspire you.

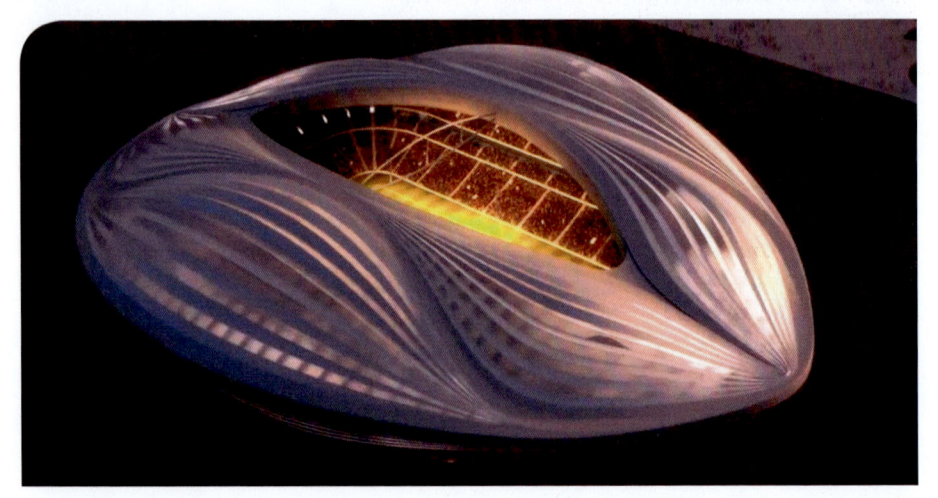

Discuss the following aspects of the design of the stadium with a partner.

1. What do the curved fluid lines of the building suggest about Qatar and its desert setting?
2. Why do you think the stadium is designed as roofless and open?
3. What impression do the colours of the building make?
4. Overall, do you think the design is successful in encouraging football fans to want to visit this place as the first Middle Eastern country to host the World Cup?

6 Evaluation

1. Read the introduction to the text on page 71 again together with the last sentence of paragraph one. This sentence establishes the genre of this story. It engages the reader by suggesting the setting is not quite as cosy as it first seemed.

    a. What significant event is introduced in the sub-extract above?

    b. Explain how this changes the mood of the text.

    c. Explain how this changes the reader's expectations of what is to follow.

    d. Explain why the writer's choice of settings works well for the opening of a ghost story. Give reasons for your answer.

2. Consider the annotated text below. Notice how the student has identified significant incidents and events in this section that contribute to the mood of the story.

event – new character – shocking/surprising

incident – girl's actions – shocking; idea of distress

idea – desperation, upset

incident of Miss R acting, upset

idea of concern, worry

> I turned towards the long, narrow windows, and there, sure enough, I saw a little girl, less than my Miss Rosamond dressed all unfit to be out-of-doors such a bitter night – crying, and beating against the window-panes, as if she wanted to be let in. She seemed to sob and wail, till Miss Rosamond could bear it no longer, and was flying to the door to open it,

Use a printout of the extract to mark two further incidents/ideas that are introduced. Note how they affect the overall mood of the story. Alternatively, copy and extend the table below. Use the annotations above as a model.

Idea/Incident	Mood of the story
Nurse saw the girl	Shock, surprise
Girl crying and beating	Shock, distress
Miss R flying to door	Desperation

3. Complete the student's paragraph below in answer to the question:

    > 'Evaluate the success of the ideas and incidents in establishing the mood of this ghost story. Use evidence to support your answer.'

    The opening of this section establishes a sudden change in mood as the nurse's game with the child changes on the appearance of the little girl at the window. This incident is shocking especially as it reminds the reader of the girl that no one believes exists and the mood becomes disturbed. Her actions of 'crying and beating'...

6.3 Evaluating ideas, incidents and events

Narrative prose* is built through the telling of things that happen which may in turn introduce new ideas. These things might be big or small. For example, a small idea or incident might be a new issue or topic introduced by a character or narrator*, the appearance of someone new, or a significant action carried out by a character. A bigger event might also be introduced, such as a fire or a major announcement.

> **English terms**
>
> *****Narrative prose:** The telling of a story, written in continuous prose rather than poetry
>
> *****Narrator:** The person who tells the story

Activity 4

Read the first paragraph and one more paragraph from *The Old Nurse's Story*, below.

Earlier in the story, the little girl ran away from home in the snow and nearly died of the cold; she told the family she had followed a little girl who beckoned her further into the cold, but no one believes her.

> And so it happened, that one afternoon, not long before Christmas day, we were playing together on the billiard-table in the great hall (not that we knew the right way of playing, but she liked to roll the smooth ivory balls with her pretty hands, and I liked to do whatever she did); and, by-and-by, without our noticing it, it grew dusk indoors, though it was still light in the open air, and I was thinking of taking her back into the nursery, when, all of a sudden, she cried out, – 'Look, Hester! Look! There is my poor little girl out in the snow!'
>
> I turned towards the long, narrow windows, and there, sure enough, I saw a little girl, less than my Miss Rosamond dressed all unfit to be out-of-doors such a bitter night – crying, and beating against the window-panes, as if she wanted to be let in. She seemed to sob and wail, till Miss Rosamond could bear it no longer, and was flying to the door to open it, when, all of a sudden, and close upon us, the great organ pealed out so loud and thundering, it fairly made me tremble; and all the more, when I remembered me that, even in the stillness of that dead-cold weather, I had heard no sound of little battering hands upon the window-glass, although the Phantom Child had seemed to put forth all its force; and, although I had seen it wail and cry, no faintest touch of sound had fallen upon my ears. Whether I remembered all this at the very moment, I do not know; the great organ sound had so stunned me into terror; but this I know, I caught up Miss Rosamond before she got the hall-door opened, and clutched her, and carried her away, kicking and screaming, into the large, bright kitchen, where Dorothy and Agnes were busy with their mince-pies.

6 Evaluation

Activity 2

Work with a partner to pair the settings in column 1 ('Setting') with the most suitable literary genres and themes in column 2 ('Genre'). Links for one setting have been shown as a guide.

Setting	Genre
A mansion	Romance
A country garden	Detective fiction
A castle	Family saga
A boarding school	Horror story
A police station	Ghost story
A wood	War story
A cottage	Childhood story

How might these settings change if adjectives are added? Try using 'warm' or 'dark' in front of each one. Discuss with a partner if this changes your choices.

Activity 3

Extract from *The Old Nurse's Story* by Elizabeth Gaskell

Now read a paragraph from the short story *The Old Nurse's Story* by Elizabeth Gaskell. The nurse describes an afternoon with her charge, an orphaned upper-class girl called Miss Hester Rosamond.

> And so it happened, that one afternoon, not long before Christmas day, we were playing together on the billiard-table in the great hall (not that we knew the right way of playing, but she liked to roll the smooth ivory balls with her pretty hands, and I liked to do whatever she did); and, by-and-by, without our noticing it, it grew dusk indoors, though it was still light in the open air, and I was thinking of taking her back into the nursery, when...

1. What is the setting of this paragraph?
2. What mood* or atmosphere* is created by this setting? Use quotations to support your answer.
3. What kind of story might you expect from such a setting? Give reasons for your answer.

English term

***Mood* or *Atmosphere*:** The feelings that a text creates for the reader, conveyed through language choice

6.2 Text aspects: Setting, Ideas and Incidents, Themes and Events

Evaluating a piece of writing is similar to judging the impact of a well-designed building. You must read the whole text and consider the overall effect a writer is aiming for. You then need to consider how well aspects of **setting**, **ideas and incidents**, **themes** and **events** in the text achieve this overall impact. In exam conditions, you are told the overall effect so your task is to consider how well the writer has achieved this.

Two useful acronyms can be made from the following words:

Setting, **I**ncidents, **T**hemes and **E**vents.

These acronyms can help you to evaluate the writer's construction of the text.

SITE – a reminder of the writer as an architect

or

TIES – a reminder about the elements used by the writer to tie together the big idea

Evaluating setting

Evaluating setting means identifying the writer's chosen setting(s) and judging its success in contributing to the text's overall impact on the reader.

The setting of prose fiction describes where and when things occur.

A setting may be chosen by a writer to create a particular mood or atmosphere, or to change it. Of course the writer can draw on a reader's expectations of a particular setting to establish a certain atmosphere, or mislead the reader by introducing a surprising event in an unexpected setting.

6.4 Evaluating themes

A theme is a topic that runs throughout a text, such as love, power, violence, the supernatural, death. A theme is often reflected in the vocabulary that is used within the text; a network of words linked to that theme can be identified.

Consider how themes contribute to the effectiveness of a story. Read the end of the extract from *The Old Nurse's Story* before completing the activities on page 74.

> 'What is the matter with my sweet one?' cried Dorothy, as I bore* in Miss Rosamond, who was sobbing as if her heart would break.
>
> 'She won't let me open the door for my little girl to come in; and she'll die if she is out on the Fells all night. Cruel, naughty Hester,' she said, slapping me; but she might have struck harder, for I had seen a look of ghastly terror on Dorothy's face, which made my very blood run cold.
>
> 'Shut the back kitchen door fast, and bolt it well,' said she to Agnes. She said no more; she gave me raisins and almonds to quiet Miss Rosamond: but she sobbed about the little girl in the snow, and would not touch any of the good things. I was thankful when she cried herself to sleep in bed. Then I stole down to the kitchen, and told Dorothy I had made up my mind I would carry my darling back to my father's house in Applethwaite; where, if we lived humbly, we lived at peace. I said I had been frightened enough with the old lord's organ-playing; but now that I had seen for myself this little, moaning child, all decked out as no child in the neighbourhood could be, beating and battering to get in, yet always without any sound or noise – with the dark wound on its right shoulder; and that Miss Rosamond had known it again for the phantom that had nearly lured her to her death (which Dorothy knew was true); I would stand it no longer.
>
> I saw Dorothy change colour once or twice. When I had done, she told me she did not think I could take Miss Rosamond with me, for that she was my lord's ward*, and I had no right over her; and she asked me, would I leave the child that I was so fond of, just for sounds and sights that could do me no harm.

> **Examiner tip**
>
> Read the question on evaluation carefully to be sure you have identified the focus of your answer.

> **Glossary**
>
> *__Bore:__ Carried
>
> *__Ward:__ Person, especially a child, who is dependent upon the care and support of an appointed guardian

6 Evaluation

Activity 5

A theme runs across a whole extract. To complete the activities below you will just focus on the final part of the extract, which appears on the previous page. However, you will need to draw on your knowledge of the plot from the earlier part of the extract and the introduction to the story (see page 71).

1. Look at the themes below. Select three which you consider to be most relevant to the extract on page 73. Use what you know about the earlier passage and from the introduction.

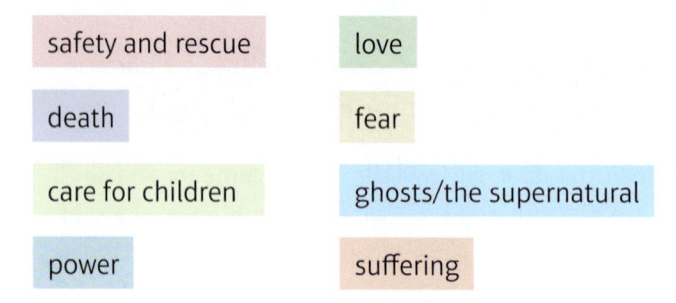

   safety and rescue   love

   death   fear

   care for children   ghosts/the supernatural

   power   suffering

2. Find quotations from the text extract to reflect each theme you choose. Consider each theme by commenting on your quotations, linking them with events in this extract and earlier in the story. One example is shown below.

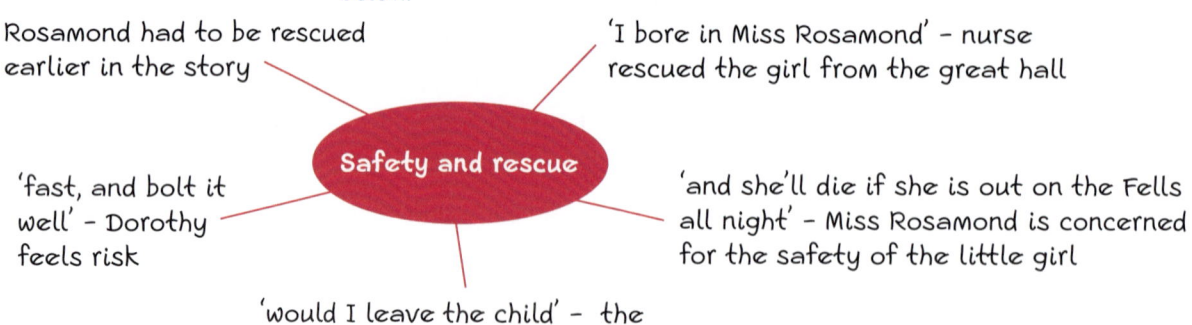

   Rosamond had to be rescued earlier in the story

   'I bore in Miss Rosamond' – nurse rescued the girl from the great hall

   'fast, and bolt it well' – Dorothy feels risk

   Safety and rescue

   'and she'll die if she is out on the Fells all night' – Miss Rosamond is concerned for the safety of the little girl

   'would I leave the child' – the nurse's role is protective of Miss R

3. Use your notes from task 2 above to evaluate the writer's use of themes in answer to the following question.

   > 'Evaluate how successfully the writer uses themes to convey a sense of horror in *The Old Nurse's Story*.'

   Focus your answer on the extract on the previous page. Use quotations to support your judgements about the writer's success.

   Use the following sentence as a starter to begin your response.

   > Gaskell uses various themes in the story to successfully convey increasing horror. In the first paragraph, where the nurse carries Miss Rosamond into the kitchen…

Examiner tip

Remember to use words that indicate you are making a positive judgement of how setting, incidents, themes and events are working. For example:

successfully   skilfully

effectively   works well

6.5 Writing evaluatively

Remembering the acronym SITE will allow you to check which of these aspects are being used by the writer as the text progresses to achieve an overall effect.

Activity 6

Skim through each paragraph of the full extract from *The Old Nurse's Story* on pages 71 and 73 and think about which aspects of 'SITE' are most significant.

Below is the opening of a response to the following question on the extract.

> 'In this extract the writer tries to convey the experience of being threatened by the supernatural. Evaluate how the writer does this well, using references from the text to support your answer.'

Read the model answer on page 76. The student has evaluated the first paragraph of the extract on page 71, up to 'when all of a sudden'. As you read, complete the following tasks.

1. Identify which aspects of SITE are addressed, in each paragraph of the student response.

2. Identify which aspects of SITE are most focused on in this response on the next page.

3. List the evaluative vocabulary that highlights the student's judgements.

4. Read the teacher's comments on the student's response.

6 Evaluation

Annotation	Text
considers setting	Overall in this extract the writer successfully shows how adults and children react to strange events and how the supernatural can affect even the most privileged places. The writer begins this extract by successfully establishing a warm and cosy setting within a rich home. References to 'the billiard-table in the great hall' and the date just before Christmas make the reader feel comfortable and there is no sense of threat. This effectively creates a feeling of comfort which is broken by Miss Rosamond's sudden speech which shows her surprise at seeing the ghost: 'when, all of a sudden, she cried out'. In this way, threat of the supernatural works well as it is a sudden shock for the reader and the characters.

Annotations pointing to the first paragraph:
- considers setting
- uses short embedded quotations
- links to the question focus
- evaluative term
- incident/issue
- evaluative term

The event of the face appearing at the window and the actions of the ghostly child continue this idea. The nurse's worry about the child being outside and the fact that Miss Rosamond expresses care for the girl emphasise the threat that the ghost poses. At this point in the story, the two settings of inside and outside the house offer some safety for the characters inside, but the fact that the ghost is close by and looking in increase the threat since before this point the nurse did not believe that the little girl existed. The 'crying, and beating' of the ghostly child on the window work well to indicate some desperation which suggests there may be a threat to Miss Rosamond's safety.

Annotations pointing to the second paragraph:
- event
- incident/issue
- incident/issue
- focuses on the question
- moves through the text chronologically
- setting
- focuses on the question
- incident/issue
- short relevant quotation

76

6.6 Evaluating non-fiction

The evaluation skills you have practised for prose fiction are transferable to non-fiction. However, there are a few extra learning points.

When evaluating a non-fiction text, you can use the acronym TAPS to establish:

Text type – is it journalism (for example an article or review), a speech, from a journal or reference book extract, autobiography, letter, obituary or travel writing?

Audience – who is the reader? Is it a particular social group? Is it the general public?

Purpose* – what is the text for? It may have a combination of purposes. For example, to inform, persuade, explain, argue, describe or entertain.

Source – where is it from? Notice where and when it was written. This will give you information about context which can help you to understand the background to the text and perhaps its writer.

For prose fiction, you practised the use of SITE to consider setting, ideas, themes and events to evaluate the text. You can also use this method to evaluate non-fiction. You need to understand how it transfers to very different styles of text, for example speeches, journals, reference book extracts, autobiography, letters, obituaries and travel writing.

English terms

*Purpose: The overall aim of a text

*Anecdotes: Real life stories or examples

Using SITE for Evaluation

Setting: What is the context of the piece? Is it written recently or from a much earlier time period? Is it referring to particular time periods or places?

Ideas and **T**hemes: What themes and ideas are raised by the writer? Are different ideas and viewpoints introduced, drawing on others' views? Are ideas and themes supported or developed by anecdotes* or examples?

Events: Are there factual events reported, that develop the main ideas? Are there anecdotes or true stories that are used?

Examiner tip

The mark scheme for evaluation lists **S**etting, **I**deas, **T**hemes and **E**vents. You do not need to be overly concerned about using these words in your response or worry about whether something is a theme or an idea. Use SITE as a general check to stand back to judge the writer's success.

6 Evaluation

Activity 7

Extract from 'Big Ben to be silenced for months by tower and clock repairs'

Read the beginning of the non-fiction news article below. With a partner, establish the text type, audience, purpose and source.

Big Ben to be silenced for months by tower and clock repairs

Restoration of the Elizabeth Tower, which houses the huge bell, expected to start in early 2017

Tuesday 26 April 2016

Big Ben is to fall silent while urgent repair works are carried out on the Elizabeth Tower and the famous clock, the House of Commons has announced.

The bell will be silenced for several months as part of a £29m programme to repair the clock faces and mechanism as well as cracks in the tower's masonry and corrosion in the roof.

Activity 8

Now consider a student's annotations of this text to evaluate how well the writer conveys important news information to the reader.

Identify a quotation from the newspaper text to illustrate each element.

1. **S** – the modern reader is given historical information about the clock and tower

   Quotation _____

2. **I** – the idea of the political importance of the building is emphasised

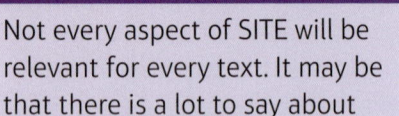

   Quotation _____

3. **T** – the theme of repairs and restoration is introduced, which is developed by a range of facts and costs

   Quotation _____

4. **E** – the expected moment of the bell's silence is conveyed as something significant and different in terms of London's history

   Quotation _____

> **Examiner tip**
>
> Not every aspect of SITE will be relevant for every text. It may be that there is a lot to say about **I**deas and less to say about **E**vents for example.

6.7 Writing an evaluation response

Letter from the BBC 'Big Ben's Bongs (lack of)'

Once you have identified the **T**ext type, **A**udience, **P**urpose and **S**ource of a non-fiction text, and annotated any key features of **SITE** in chronological order, you are ready to begin writing.

Read the text 'Big Ben's Bongs (lack of)' on page 80, written by a BBC Editor in response to a letter from a young girl offering to replace Big Ben's missing chimes on the news with her own. Think carefully about the Editor's intentions* in responding to the girl. The writer wants to say 'no' kindly. How well does he manage this?

Activity 9

1. Identify the TAPS of the text on page 80.

   Text type _____

   Audience _____

   Purpose _____

   Source _____

2. Work with a partner to anchor your reading of 'Big Ben's Bongs (lack of)' and identify elements of SITE, preferably using a printout of the text. The first paragraph is annotated for you.

> **English term**
>
> *****Intention:** The impact and effect that the writer wants the text to have on the reader

> **Examiner tip**
>
> Include appropriate short quotations from the text you are evaluating to support the points you make in your judgement.

> **Examiner tip**
>
> Remember that SITE is just a method to help you evaluate. Some aspects may be more frequent than others, you may not need to comment on each paragraph.

6 Evaluation

British Broadcasting Corporation W1 NBH 03C, BBC Broadcasting House, Portland Place, London W1A 1AA
Telephone +44 20 361 41444   Email wato@bbc.co.uk pm@bbc.co.uk bh@bbc.co.uk

BBC

The World at One, PM, Broadcasting House & The World this Weekend

Miss Phoebe Elizabeth Hanson,   12th December 2016

Re. Big Ben's Bongs (lack of)

Dear Miss Hanson,

Thank you for your letter and for your very imaginative idea about what to do when Big Ben falls silent for repairs early next year. Some of the cleverest and most important people at the BBC are scratching their heads, wondering quite what to do.

Once before, when Big Ben fell silent for repairs, we played different birdsong every evening. The listeners loved that. Then the people behind Tweet of the Day (that's on each day just before 6 in the morning) stole our idea... so we can't do that again.

I must say I was very much taken with your idea... and have passed it on to those who make the decisions. As you know, the Bongs are live... and (you may not know this) the beginning of the Westminster Chimes (the bit that goes BimBom BimBom BimBobBimBom before the first BOOONNNGGGGGGGGGG!) is always at a slightly different time (which is why you sometimes hear someone accidentally talking when they start). It depends on things like temperature and atmospheric pressure and stuff like that.

So it would be quite a task for you, doing the Bongs: you'd have to rush in after school each day (and at the weekend), rush home for tea, homework, a bit of chillin', then a quick sleep. And then – here's the hard bit – you'd have to rush back in again at midnight, because there are live bongs again before the midnight news. That's an awful lot of work for someone who is still quite young. I know I wouldn't like to do all that.

Thank you very much for writing to us. I'm very impressed that you listen to Radio 4. I wish my two children did.

Have a spiffing Christmas and a stupendous and lucky 2017.

Roger Sawyer
Editor: PM, Broadcasting House, iPM – BBC Radio 4

S – refers to the context – it is a response to a previous letter

T – theme of praise for the young child and her suggestions runs throughout

I – idea of the silence resulting from the clock's repairs is established as fact

S – the professional business context of the BBC is established

6.8 Considering language and structure to support evaluation

To evaluate a text you will need to select evidence from it. You should use textual references to support your judgements. However, you must remember to focus on 'how well' the writer achieves their aim, rather than just 'how', as you did on Language and Structure work.

Activity 10

1. The word and phrase banks in the table below reflect the language of the BBC letter. Copy and complete the table by finding relevant quotations from the source text.

Humorous language	Words of praise
Stole	Cleverest
Scratching their heads	Most important

2. With a partner agree how each word bank contributes to the success of the piece. Think carefully about how each one contributes to the writer's tone*, or register*.

3. Write a paragraph evaluating how each category of words contributes to the success of this letter. Use the sentence starters below to help you:

   The writer's use of humorous words adds to the success of this text. The effect of these is to [skilfully/cleverly/smoothly]...

English terms

*Tone: The way a writer expresses a certain attitude or mood through their language choices

*Register: The language used to create a style of writing, or used by a certain group of people (formal or informal)

Examiner tip

Tone is looked at in more depth in Unit 7.

Activity 11

Consider how the writer has organised his letter, as outlined in the headings below.

- Paragraph 1: Thank you
- Paragraph 2: What's happened in the past
- Paragraph 3: The technical issues of the 'Bongs'
- Paragraph 4: The reasons her suggestion is not possible
- Paragraphs 5 and 6: Friendly sign off

1. Read the text again in the light of the headings above. Discuss with a partner why this structure works well in kindly refusing the girl's suggestion.

2. Write a paragraph using this information to explain how the writer successfully achieves this refusal using structure. The focus must be on 'how well' rather than 'how'. Use the sentence starter below to begin:

   The writer successfully structures the text to enable him to refuse the girl's offer in the kindest possible way...

Mini Assessment 1 – prose fiction

Assessment objective
- Evaluate texts critically and support this with appropriate textual references (AO4)

Examiner tip

Remember that one or more elements of SITE may be relevant. You need to have understood the whole extract. You can be selective about what you think is most important: you do not need to write about every paragraph from the extract.

Examiner tip

The mark scheme for evaluation lists **S**etting, **I**deas, **T**hemes and **E**vents. You do not need to be overly concerned about using these words in your response or worry about whether something is a theme or an idea. Use SITE as a general check to stand back to judge the writer's success.

The skills you have secured in this section focus on evaluating texts critically with appropriate textual references.

The assessment below will allow you to test your skills and review your progress in this area in preparation for exam-focused work.

1. Read the full extract from *The Old Nurse's Story* again.

2. Continue the student response on pages 75–76, to add two or three more paragraphs of evaluation in relation to the question:

   > 'In this extract the writer tries to convey the experience of being threatened by the supernatural. Evaluate how successfully this is achieved, using references from the text to support your answer.'

3. If you are working on a printout, annotate each paragraph from the phrase 'When all of a sudden' to the end before answering the question, to identify where the writer has used SITE in relation to the question focus 'threat from the supernatural'. Otherwise, jot down your ideas on paper.

4. Check your work for:
   - evaluative language
   - written accuracy
   - relevant short quotations
   - links with the question focus of 'being threatened'.

Self-assessment

Look back at the work you have done in the first part of this unit. You can now review your performance of the skills you have practised using *The Old Nurse's story*.

Skill	🟢 🟠 🔴
I can identify and analyse setting, ideas, themes and events in prose fiction texts.	
I can offer informed critical judgements about a prose fiction text.	
I can select appropriate and detailed references from a prose fiction text.	
I can evaluate the contribution of textual evidence to the success of a prose fiction text.	

Mini Assessment 2 – non-fiction

The assessment below will allow you to test your skills and review your progress in this area in preparation for exam-focused work.

1. Read the text 'Big Ben's Bongs (lack of)' again together with your evaluative annotations of the Setting, Ideas, Themes and Events.

2. Write three paragraphs in response to the following question:

   > 'Evaluate how successfully the editor manages to refuse the girl's offer of help.'

   Remember to include a short comment on how language and structure contribute to the text's success.

3. Check your work for:
   - written accuracy
   - relevant short quotations
   - links to the question focus
   - evaluative language.

Self-assessment

Look back at the work you have done in this unit. You can now review your performance of the skills you have practised using 'Big Ben's Bongs (lack of)'.

The skills for AO4 (Evaluate) that you have practised in this unit are specifically tested in Paper 1 question 4 and Paper 2 question 6.

Skill	🟢 🟠 🔴
I can identify and analyse setting, ideas, themes and events in non-fiction texts.	
I can offer informed critical judgements about a non-fiction text.	
I can select appropriate and detailed references from a non-fiction text.	
I can evaluate the contribution of textual evidence to the success of a non-fiction text.	

7 Word and sentence choices

Writing

Assessment objective
- To experiment with varying sentence length using a variety of conjunctions (Relates to AO6)

Assessment links
English Language Paper 1 questions 5 or 6 and Paper 2 questions 8 or 9.

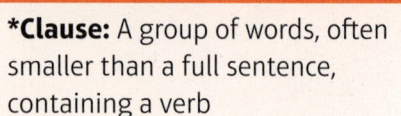

English terms
*Clause: A group of words, often smaller than a full sentence, containing a verb

*Conjunction: A word used to connect clauses or sentences (for example, 'and', 'if', 'but')

7.1 Sentence length: the long and the short of it

One of the choices writers face when completing a piece of writing is how long or short to make each sentence. Both short and long sentences are useful in different types of writing. Varying sentence length can help to keep the reader interested, and create different effects.

The simplest sort of sentence has only one clause*. There is an example of a clause in Activity 1: 'She's going to regret that error.'

However, just because a sentence is simple does not mean it can't be very effective. In fact, very short sentences can be a good 'shock tactic' to keep the reader on their toes, giving variety in how the writing is structured. It is quite common for writers to use single-word sentences.

Activity 1

1. Discuss why the writer of these extracts has used one-word sentences.

   She's going to regret that error. Massively.

   What an idiotic thing to say. Unbelievable.

2. What effect do you think the writer is trying to convey? Give reasons for your answer.

Using conjunctions

More complex sentences will often have more than one clause. One way in which writers join together multi-clause sentences is by using conjunctions*. These are words that join clauses or sentences together.

It is likely that the first conjunction you learned when you started to write was 'and'. However, it is important to use different words to join clauses, so your writing does not sound too boring or repetitive. Think of other words you could use, and remember you can also use punctuation marks to replace 'and'.

Examiner tip
AO6 requires you to use a variety of sentence structures. In the exam, leave time to read through your finished work to check that you have met this objective.

Activity 2

1. Rewrite the paragraph on the following page, replacing every instance of 'and' with a different conjunction or an appropriate punctuation mark. Avoid using the same conjunction too many times. Look at the conjunctions in the table below to help you.

so	because	whereas	before	where	although	since	as
while	if	unless	until	however	but	despite	

7.1 Sentence length: the long and the short of it

> We walked down to the football ground and all around us from the surrounding streets fans were funnelling down to the stadium and my friend bought a burger and then we went in and stood on the terrace. We couldn't see very well and we moved to empty seats higher up and then it was nearly kickoff. The atmosphere was building and all around us there was a wall of sound and when the teams came on to the pitch our side of the ground roared their approval and the opposition fans couldn't be heard. Our players were really up for it and so was the crowd and the team attacked relentlessly. The other team struggled with our pace and intensity and kept giving the ball away and we won easily and my friend and I said we thought this year could be our year.

2. Once you have rewritten the paragraph, read the new version and decide if it sounds more interesting.

Activity 3

For these tasks, work in groups of three. You will each need a blank sheet of paper.

1. Write a simple clause on your piece of paper. For example, 'Samira was watching television'. Do not put a full stop after the last word.

2. Pass your piece of paper to the person on your right. Each of you must now use a conjunction to add a second clause to the sentence. For example, 'Samira was watching television **when** suddenly the room went dark'. You can use any of the conjunctions from the table in Activity 2.

3. Pass the paper again to the person on your right. Each of you must complete the multi-clause sentence using a conjunction from the table below, before adding a final clause. For example, 'Samira was watching television **when** suddenly the room went dark **although** it was a bright, sunny day outside'.

as soon as	in order that	even though
just in case	in spite of	just as
as if	in order to	yet

4. Finally, pass the paper to the right one last time. Read the short stories aloud. What differences have the conjunctions made?

5. Repeat the process. This time, you must not use a conjunction that was used in the first round, but you may use a punctuation mark to separate the clauses. This should lead to some even more interesting stories.

Examiner tip

Analysis of students' writing at GCSE shows that many students restrict themselves to using only the most common conjunctions, such as 'and' and 'but'. Students achieving the higher grades tend to use more unusual or complex conjunctions.

7 Word and sentence choices

> **Assessment objective**
> - To understand what verbs are and to use them to create effect in your own writing
> - To understand how to use simple language to create effect
>
> (Relates to AO6)

7.2 Verb choice: re-verbing

The great American writer Ernest Hemingway was famous for saying that the best writing was often the simplest writing. He said that he always tried to cut away any 'ornamentation' from his writing. By this, he meant not using unnecessary description (too many adjectives or adverbs) and only using simple punctuation and words with few syllables.

Extract from *A Farewell to Arms* by Ernest Hemingway

In this novel, the protagonist*, Frederic Henry, is serving in the American army in Italy during the First World War.

> The forest of oak trees on the mountain beyond the town was gone. The forest had been green in the summer when we had come into the town but now there were the stumps and the broken trunks and the ground torn up, and one day at the end of the fall when I was out where the oak forest had been I saw a cloud coming over the mountain. It came very fast and the sun went a dull yellow and then everything was gray and the sky was covered and the cloud came on down the mountain and suddenly we were in it and it was snow.

> **English term**
>
> *****Protagonist:** The main character in a novel

Notice how many words Hemingway uses in the extract that have more than two syllables. How many commas does he use? How many times does he use 'the' and 'and'?

Activity 4

1. Read the student answer below, which is the opening to a narrative written by a student in their exam. There is a lot of 'ornamentation'. For example, the opening sentence uses two adverbs, 'intently' and 'firmly', to modify the verb 'looked'.

> He looked intently and firmly into the mirror. He swooped his fingers gently and delicately through his hair and grabbed his tie harshly to straighten it. "Looking good," he almost said out loud to himself but didn't. His client was sitting uncomfortably and low down in an expensive leather office chair. He coughed loudly and roughly and when this didn't get any reaction from Leroy he did it again. The detective spun round swiftly and hurriedly on the heel of his expensive hand-made Italian shoes.
> "Are we going to talk properly about the case or are you going to spend the rest of the time staring and gazing at yourself in the mirror?"
> The detective showed absolutely no sort of emotion but simply commented, "Patience is a virtue", and then he turned quickly back to look with great care and concentration at his reflection.

2. Rewrite the extract to edit it down. Try to:
   - cut out words or phrases you think are unnecessary
   - change some of the verbs to give a clearer picture to the reader.

7.2 Verb choice: re-verbing

Simple or varied?

Now, Hemingway had the advantage of not having to write for a GCSE exam in which you are tested on how well you can 'use a range of vocabulary and sentence structures'. When writing for your exam, it will be important to show that you can use different sentence lengths, varied vocabulary and verb* choices, and conjunctions. However, the Hemingway example does illustrate that choosing your words and sentences carefully is often more important than writing too much and in too complicated a way.

Use of verbs

Verbs are a class of word often used to describe an action, state or occurrence. It is critical that you select the most effective verbs when you are writing, to keep your writing concise and effective. It is much better to use the right verb in the first place, than to add two or three adverbs to try to increase its effect. Let's look at a sentence to explore this idea further.

> I went down the station platform towards the fight.

The verb 'went' doesn't give much information about **how** the person is moving along the platform. We could add an adverb, like 'quickly', to tell the reader more, or we could change the verb. So, we might say:

> I tore down the platform towards the fight.

OR

> I bustled down the platform towards the fight.

OR

> I mooched down the platform towards the fight.

Each of these verbs gives a different feel to the person's movement and therefore their feelings about the fight.

Activity 5

1. Change the underlined verb in each of these sentences to give the reader a clearer impression of the scene.

   - Sumitra looked at her brother across the table.
   - The dog barked at the stranger.
   - A car drove up to the very edge of the pavement.

2. Swap your work with a partner. Each of you must now change the verb again – try to choose verbs that alter the feel of the sentence.

> **Examiner tip**
> Students often think adjectives are the only way of creating descriptive effect in their writing, but other word classes, such as verbs, can also be used for this purpose.

> **English term**
> *Verb: A word used to describe an action, state or occurrence

7 Word and sentence choices

> **Assessment objective**
>
> - To understand tone, and how it can be used in different types of writing (Relates to AO5)

> **English term**
>
> ***Tone:** The way a writer expresses a certain attitude or mood through their language choices

7.3 Writing tone: watch your tone!

An important choice that writers face when writing anything, from a letter to a newspaper to a love poem, is what sort of tone* they want to use. Authors can use a particular tone to influence their readers. This is often referred to as the 'voice' of the writer.

The tone you use will differ depending on the purpose of your writing. If you are writing a letter to a newspaper to object to the building of a new housing estate in your area, the tone is probably going to be angry or determined. If you are writing a ghost story, the tone will be creepy or mysterious.

A writer's choice of words helps to create the tone of a piece of writing. The table below shows the wide range of tones that might be used in different sorts of writing and for different audiences. This will help you to identify the range of tones in the work of other writers, as well as those you can include in your own writing.

Formal or **informal**	**Humorous** or **serious**	**Polite**, restrained, measured	**Upset**, hurt, pained
Scary, afraid, alarmed	**Bored**, apathetic, weary	**Confused**, baffled, puzzled	**Sarcastic**, cynical, provocative
Dejected, gloomy, miserable	**Annoyed**, cross, exasperated	**Angry**, enraged, fuming, furious	**Dramatic**, melodramatic, over-the-top
Cheerful, jovial, light-hearted	**Tense**, agitated, uneasy	**Enthusiastic**, passionate, eager	**Shocked**, staggered, stunned

As well as the specific words used in a piece of writing, tone can also be expressed in other ways. Think about formal and informal language in general throughout your writing. Would you use the same register* in a letter to a grandparent as you would to your best friend, for example?

> **English term**
>
> ***Register:** The language used to create a style of writing, or used by a certain group of people (formal or informal)

Activity 6

1. Working with a partner, decide how you would describe the tone or voice of each of the extracts at the top of page 89, using words from the table above to help you. You can choose more than one word if you want to.

7.3 Writing tone: watch your tone!

A A strange howling noise came from the throat of this monstrous figure, and it seemed upon the point of rushing upon Mr. Marchdale. Suddenly, then, as if some impulse had seized upon it, it uttered a wild and terrible shrieking kind of laugh; and then turning, dashed through the window, and in one instant disappeared from before the eyes of those who felt nearly annihilated by its fearful presence. (*Varney the Vampire*)

B 'What is the matter with my sweet one?' cried Dorothy, as I bore in Miss Rosamond, who was sobbing as if her heart would break. (*The Old Nurse's Story*, E Gaskell)

C Mr. Manson, our second mate, saw a ghost last night—or, at least, says that he did, which of course is the same thing. It is quite refreshing to have some new topic of conversation after the eternal routine of bears and whales which has served us for so many months. (*Captain of Pole Star*, Conan Doyle)

D I am so annoyed with the grown ups... they go on and on about us young ones... but it's them! Every Saturday I have to wade through old guys on their way home from the pub – unbelievable... drinking too much again...

2. When you have decided on the tone of each piece, choose two or three words or phrases from the extract that you think are most important in setting the tone.

Activity 7

1. Look carefully at the painting on the right. You are going to use this painting as a prompt for writing in a certain tone. The painting is a graffiti mural by the artist Banksy.

2. Choose one word from the table on the previous page that you think best describes the tone of the painting.

3. Write down a few more ideas about the painting – either a description of it or some ideas that the painting inspires.

4. Write a paragraph of about 200 words in the tone (or voice) you have decided on. The paragraph could be a description of the painting, or it could be a separate piece of creative writing inspired by it. Remember – your piece of writing should be a creative piece **in** your chosen tone.

5. Compare the piece you wrote with a partner. Did you try to establish a similar tone or were there differences? What difference did your word choices make?

7 Word and sentence choices

Assessment objective
- To use triples and repetition to create effect in your writing (Relates to AO6)

7.4 Am I repeating myself?: The power of triples

'You're just repeating yourself!' is usually a criticism of a person who is boring their audience by saying the same thing over and over again. But there are some occasions when repetition can actually help a piece of writing or a speech to have *more*, rather than less, impact.

Lists of three, or 'triples' as they are sometimes called, use repetition to persuade or manipulate an audience to react in the way the writer or speaker intends. Triples are more commonly known as the 'rule of three'.

A campaign encouraging people to be more environmentally conscious introduced the slogan:

> Reduce. Reuse. Recycle.

This example is a verb triple, which means it uses three verbs in succession.

Can you think of any more advertising campaigns that use triples in this way?

Phrase triples and repetition

In phrase triples, a writer uses three similar phrases in a section of writing. This kind of repetition is used to increase impact.

Extracts from speeches by Nelson Mandela and Winston Churchill

Nelson Mandela was an anti-apartheid activist and former President of South Africa. He went to jail for sabotage and spent 27 years behind bars before being released and elected as president in 1994. In a famous speech made by Nelson Mandela at his trial for sabotage in 1964, he used phrase triples to great effect to repeat and reinforce the sense of the African people fighting against a great power. Here is a short extract from his speech.

> This then is what the ANC is fighting. Our struggle is a truly national one. *It is a struggle* of the African people, inspired by our own suffering and our own experience. *It is a struggle* for the right to live. During my lifetime I have dedicated my life *to this struggle* of the African people.

Winston Churchill was the British prime minister during the Second World War, and delivered some of the most stirring speeches of recent history. The extract on the following page is from a speech given in 1940. Notice how he uses repetition of words and phrases to fire up his audience.

Examiner tip
When thinking about using techniques such as triples, make sure they fit in with and contribute to the overall effect of your text.

Nelson Mandela

7.4 Am I repeating myself?: The power of triples

We shall go on to the end. We shall fight in France, we shall fight on the seas and oceans, we shall fight with growing confidence and growing strength in the air, we shall defend our island, whatever the cost may be. We shall fight on the beaches, we shall fight on the landing grounds, we shall fight in the fields and in the streets, we shall fight in the hills; we shall never surrender...

Activity 8

1. Work with a partner. Using this extract from a speech by Winston Churchill, identify where triples or repetition have been used for effect.

We have before us an ordeal of the most grievous kind. We have before us many, many long months of struggle and of suffering. You ask, what is our policy? I will say: it is to wage war, by sea, land, and air, with all our might and with all the strength that God can give us; to wage war against a monstrous tyranny never surpassed in the dark, lamentable catalogue of human crime. That is our policy. You ask, what is our aim? I can answer in one word: it is victory, victory at all costs, victory in spite of all terror, victory, however long and hard the road may be.

Winston Churchill

2. Discuss what else makes the speeches by Mandela and Churchill effective. To help with your discussion, consider:
    - the choice of words and sentences
    - the length of sentences
    - repetition of the same words.

3. Whose speech do you think is more effective? Why?

Activity 9

Working in small groups, imagine you work for an advertising agency and have been asked to write slogans for some public information campaigns.

1. Compose a slogan of three **verb triples** to encourage the public to:
    - keep children safe online
    - keep dangerous cleaning products away from young children
    - eat less junk food.
2. Each campaign will have a leaflet to reinforce the message in the slogan. In the same teams, choose two of the campaigns and write the opening paragraphs of the leaflets using phrase triples. Use 150 words maximum for each paragraph.

7 Word and sentence choices

> **Assessment objective**
> - To use punctuation correctly so your writing is clear and has the desired effect (Relates to AO6)

> **Examiner tip**
> In the exam you must pay careful attention to your spelling, punctuation and grammar. Check your work thoroughly for accuracy to avoid losing marks.

7.5 Punctuation: making a mark – Part 1

Why is punctuation important?

The main reason why we punctuate our writing is to help the reader understand the text. Punctuation guides the reader through sentences, helping to make it clear what the writer is saying by showing when to pause, how to pronounce words and when ideas start and finish. Some punctuation marks are used at word level:

- **Hyphens [-]** are used to join two words into a compound word, for example *self-confidence* or *house-keeping*.
- **Apostrophes** are used in two ways:
  - to show that a letter has been omitted (contraction)
  - to show that something belongs to somebody (possession).

Use of apostrophe	Examples
Contraction, to replace a letter in a word or join two words together	'I **do not** want to come' becomes 'I **don't** want to come'. 'I will not walk the dog' becomes 'I **won't** walk the dog'.
To show singular possession	'Luke **Skywalker's** lightsaber' – the lightsaber belonging to Luke Skywalker.
To show plural possession	'My **parents'** house' – when the plural noun ends with 's', add an apostrophe. 'The **children's** party'– when the plural noun doesn't end with 's', use the rule of singular possession.

Activity 10

1. The extract below, from *Grey is the Colour of Hope,* a memoir written in 1988 by the Russian writer and poet Irina Ratushinskaya, has had all the punctuation removed. Rewrite it, inserting appropriate punctuation marks.

At first there was one locker for every prisoner and the surplus lockers were removed only a year later even so it was a tight squeeze try to picture it for yourself my readers go through your cupboards and wardrobes and pick out what you would consider to be the barest essentials to serve you for the next seven years dont forget to include your maximum allowance of five books letters photographs of your nearest and dearest whom you wont see for years to come stamps envelopes those treacherous underclothes a couple of towels

2. Look at the extract with the punctuation you have added. How does the punctuation add to the sense of living with the bare essentials only?

The most important punctuation marks are those that help us with sentence construction. Punctuation is a key tool for shaping and crafting writing – for example, by helping an author control the length and meaning of their sentences and thereby leading the reader through the text.

7.5 Punctuation: making a mark – Part 1

Stops and other endings

Full stops [.] mark the end of a sentence, a complete statement.

> Marie ran for the bus.

Question marks [?] and **exclamation marks [!]** are types of stop. They show that the sentence is either a question or an exclamation, rather than a statement. They also imply a change of intonation if you are reading aloud.

> Why is the dog here?

> I can't believe it!

Sentences aren't always completed. In dialogue, for example, a **dash [–]** suggests that a sentence has been interrupted in some way.

> "Wait, are you–"

An **ellipsis […]** is another way of showing that a sentence has been left in mid-air.

> "This is the end of everything…"

Commas and other dividing marks

Commas [,] are used within sentences to divide them into units that are not grammatically complete. Commas help to show the reader how the sentence is constructed and where the pauses come if you are reading the sentence aloud. Commas are also inserted between items in lists. The rules about commas are less clear than the rules about full stops; deciding when to use a comma is sometimes a matter of personal preference.

> Whale sharks, which live in tropical seas, are the largest species of fish.

> John needed eggs, flour, butter, baking soda and sugar to make a cake.

A **semi-colon [;]** can be used in place of a full stop to link two statements that are grammatically independent and related in meaning. Modern writers tend to use fewer semi-colons and more full stops, so that sentences are shorter. Semi-colons can also be used between items in lists, especially when the items are phrases rather than single words.

> I enjoy horse-riding; in fact, it's my favourite thing to do.

The main purpose of a **colon [:]** is to introduce a list, a quotation or an explanation. Only one colon should be used per sentence.

> Remember: two can play at that game.

Speech marks ["abc"] surround the words spoken directly by a character in a story. They distinguish the different voices in a single piece of writing.

> "Bobby told me 'I don't think we should make the next turning'" Tim said.

Quotation marks/inverted commas ['abc'] surround words quoted from a speaker, for example in a newspaper article. They can also be used for emphasis or to show unusual phrasing.

> Priya didn't like the man's so-called 'modern' ideas.

7 Word and sentence choices

7.5 Punctuation: making a mark – Part 2

Now that you have looked at where and when you should use certain punctuation marks in your writing, you need to explore how the use of punctuation contributes to the overall effect of a text.

Extract from *Frankenstein* by Mary Shelley

Frankenstein is a gothic novel about a young scientist, Victor Frankenstein, who creates a monster using scientific experiments.

The commentary around the extract below highlights how the author has used punctuation to contribute to the overall effect of the writing – that of a sense of horror and disgust at the monster that has been created.

- Use of question mark to emphasise the narrator's state of disbelief about the monster he has created
- Use of exclamation to express the narrator's horror and to create a minor sentence that contrasts with the very long sentence that follows
- Repeated use of exclamation mark to suggest the narrator's feelings
- Repeated use of semi-colon to help the narrator add extra descriptive detail about the monster

> How can I describe my emotions at this catastrophe, or how delineate the wretch whom with such infinite pains and care I had endeavoured to form? His limbs were in proportion, and I had selected his features as beautiful. Beautiful! – Great God! His yellow skin scarcely covered the work of muscles and arteries beneath; his hair was of a lustrous black, and flowing; his teeth of a pearly whiteness; but these luxuriances only formed a more horrid contrast with his watery eyes, that seemed almost of the same colour as the dun white sockets in which they were set, his shrivelled complexion and straight black lips.

Extract from *A Tale of Two Cities* by Charles Dickens

A Tale of Two Cities is a novel. It is set in London and Paris during the French Revolution. The main characters are Doctor Manette and his daughter, Lucie, who lives in London. In the extract, Lucie and Manette help Lucie's husband escape the Bastille prison in Paris. They do this by smuggling him out dressed as one of their friends, who takes his place as prisoner.

> "Are we not going too slowly? Can they not be induced to go faster?" asks Lucie, clinging to the old man.
>
> "It would seem like flight, my darling. I must not urge them too much; it would rouse suspicion."
>
> "Look back, look back, and see if we are pursued!"
>
> "The road is clear, my dearest. So far, we are not pursued..."
>
> Out of the open country, in again among ruinous buildings, solitary farms, dye-works, tanneries, and the like, cottages in twos and threes, avenues of leafless trees. Have these men deceived us, and taken us back by another road? Is not this the same place twice over? Thank Heaven, no. A village. Look back, look back, and see if we are pursued! Hush! the posting-house.

Examiner tip

Think about how you want your reader to react to what you are writing and then choose the most appropriate means of achieving that effect. This could be through your choice of vocabulary, use of particular punctuation or any other techniques.

7.5 Punctuation: making a mark – Part 2

Activity 11

1. Working in pairs, look at the statements below. Do you think they apply to any sections of the Dickens extract?

   a. The sentences are long and complicated.
   b. The sentences are mainly simple, with just one clause.
   c. The sentences often involve two or three parts.
   d. Minor sentences are used for dramatic effect.
   e. A lot of detailed description is packed into the longer sentences.
   f. Simple actions are expressed in simple sentences.
   g. At tense moments, the sentences become shorter and simpler.
   h. Lists within a sentence build tension.

2. There are several types of sentence, for example, exclamations, questions, statements and commands. What do your findings tell you about Dickens' use of punctuation and why this is effective?

Activity 12

1. Write your own creative piece of writing, thinking about how you can use punctuation for accuracy and effect. You could either:

   - continue the Dickens extract to describe what happens next
   - write about something entirely different.

   Before you start, ask yourself the following questions.

   - **What overall effect do you want your writing to have?**
     Do you want to create a state of tension, fear or anxiety?
   - **What techniques will you use to help achieve this effect?**
     For example, vocabulary, types and lengths of sentence, etc.
   - **How will your use of punctuation contribute to this effect?**
     For example, how will you use punctuation to create the types and lengths of sentence you are looking to include?

2. When you have finished your writing, read it to yourself or to a partner.

   - How successful you have been in creating your desired effect?
   - Underline where you think you have used techniques that work well.
   - Make a note of areas you could improve – and if you have time, improve them!

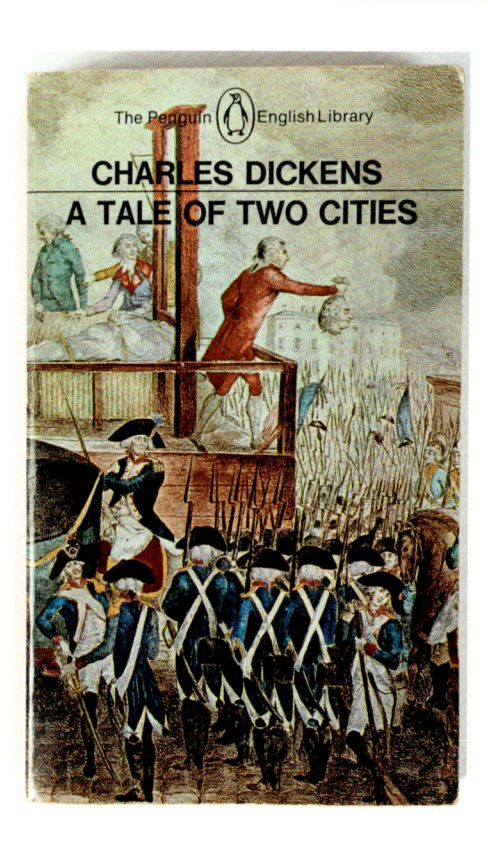

7 Word and sentence choices

Assessment objective
- Plan your writing to organise your ideas (Relates to AO5)

Examiner tip
Planning your writing is important.
- Think carefully about how you begin so that your writing is imaginative and engaging from the very start.
- Know where you will end. This will help you to write in a manner that is cohesive and coherent for your reader.
- Keep a close eye on time during the examination.

7.6 Planning

Do you get bored of being told that you must plan your writing answers in the GCSE exam? If so, you are not alone. A recent survey of the writing section of GCSE exam scripts found that fewer than 20 per cent showed any sign of planning. Those students decided they knew best and ignored the advice to plan.

It seems there is a widespread misunderstanding among students about what is important when responding to the writing questions. Many students think it is the amount they write that will help them get good marks. Consequently, examiners report every year that students are:

- writing far too much
- not spending time planning what they are going to say
- forgetting to leave enough time to check their work after they have written their answer.

If you are still writing the final sentence of your first (and only) draft at the end of the exam, you obviously haven't allowed time to check the accuracy of your spelling and punctuation. You also won't have had time to check you have used the best possible words and varied your sentence structure.

Activity 13

Imagine you are faced with the following task in an exam: 'Write about a time when you, or someone you know, helped somebody in need.'

1. Plan your answer to this question.
    - Remember that your response can be real or imagined.
    - Spend no more than 5 minutes planning your answer.
    - Think about the structure of what you want to say and the tone you want to use.
    - It may be useful to write a list of appropriate words you want to use.

2. Swap your completed plan with a partner. Is there anything they could have thought about to improve their plan?

Activity 11

1. Working in pairs, look at the statements below. Do you think they apply to any sections of the Dickens extract?

    a. The sentences are long and complicated.

    b. The sentences are mainly simple, with just one clause.

    c. The sentences often involve two or three parts.

    d. Minor sentences are used for dramatic effect.

    e. A lot of detailed description is packed into the longer sentences.

    f. Simple actions are expressed in simple sentences.

    g. At tense moments, the sentences become shorter and simpler.

    h. Lists within a sentence build tension.

2. There are several types of sentence, for example, exclamations, questions, statements and commands. What do your findings tell you about Dickens' use of punctuation and why this is effective?

Activity 12

1. Write your own creative piece of writing, thinking about how you can use punctuation for accuracy and effect. You could either:

    - continue the Dickens extract to describe what happens next
    - write about something entirely different.

    Before you start, ask yourself the following questions.

    - **What overall effect do you want your writing to have?**
      Do you want to create a state of tension, fear or anxiety?
    - **What techniques will you use to help achieve this effect?**
      For example, vocabulary, types and lengths of sentence, etc.
    - **How will your use of punctuation contribute to this effect?**
      For example, how will you use punctuation to create the types and lengths of sentence you are looking to include?

2. When you have finished your writing, read it to yourself or to a partner.

    - How successful you have been in creating your desired effect?
    - Underline where you think you have used techniques that work well.
    - Make a note of areas you could improve – and if you have time, improve them!

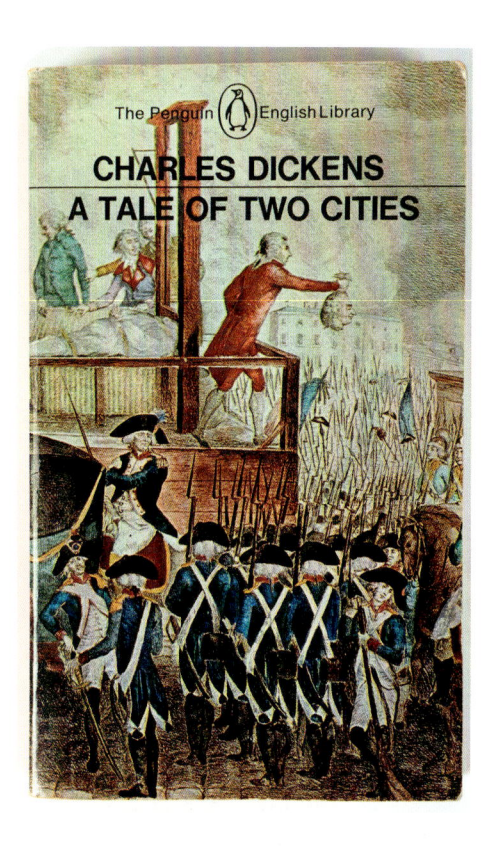

7 Word and sentence choices

> **Assessment objective**
> - Plan your writing to organise your ideas
>   (Relates to AO5)

> **Examiner tip**
> Planning your writing is important.
> - Think carefully about how you begin so that your writing is imaginative and engaging from the very start.
> - Know where you will end. This will help you to write in a manner that is cohesive and coherent for your reader.
> - Keep a close eye on time during the examination.

7.6 Planning

Do you get bored of being told that you must plan your writing answers in the GCSE exam? If so, you are not alone. A recent survey of the writing section of GCSE exam scripts found that fewer than 20 per cent showed any sign of planning. Those students decided they knew best and ignored the advice to plan.

It seems there is a widespread misunderstanding among students about what is important when responding to the writing questions. Many students think it is the amount they write that will help them get good marks. Consequently, examiners report every year that students are:

- writing far too much
- not spending time planning what they are going to say
- forgetting to leave enough time to check their work after they have written their answer.

If you are still writing the final sentence of your first (and only) draft at the end of the exam, you obviously haven't allowed time to check the accuracy of your spelling and punctuation. You also won't have had time to check you have used the best possible words and varied your sentence structure.

Activity 13

Imagine you are faced with the following task in an exam: 'Write about a time when you, or someone you know, helped somebody in need.'

1. Plan your answer to this question.
   - Remember that your response can be real or imagined.
   - Spend no more than 5 minutes planning your answer.
   - Think about the structure of what you want to say and the tone you want to use.
   - It may be useful to write a list of appropriate words you want to use.

2. Swap your completed plan with a partner. Is there anything they could have thought about to improve their plan?

Mini Assessment

The skills you have secured in this section focus on planning your writing, and experimenting with different sentence lengths and conjunctions.

> **Assessment objective**
> - Plan your writing to organise your ideas (AO5)
> - Experiment with varying sentence length using a variety of conjunctions (AO6)

1. You are going to plan, write and check a piece of writing on a topic from the list below. You can choose to write:
   - a description of what you remember about your first day at school (this can be your primary school, your current school or a school you arrived at half way through your school career)
   - an article for a newspaper about something you couldn't live without
   - a letter to the head teacher of your school suggesting how your school could be improved.

2. Plan your writing.
   a. Draw four squares and number them one to four. Each square represents a paragraph.
   b. Note down one thing you are going to write about in each square.
   c. Write your opening sentence in square one. Read it again. Does it clearly introduce what you are going to write about? Does it start with a capital letter and finish with a full-stop or another appropriate sentence ending, like a question mark?

   The diagram below shows an example plan.

1	New school uniform/walking with mum/ seeing other children **First sentence** I wasn't sure if I was going to like school.	2	Meeting class/meeting best friend Sarah – she asked if I wanted to play with her at break time/how this made me feel.
3	A description of my teacher, Mr. Hall. Brown hair, very friendly.	4	What I learned on my first day.

3. Write your essay.
   a. Write the first paragraph, using your opening sentence and adding four or five more sentences.
   b. Re-read your work. Are commas and full-stops in the right place? Have you used capital letters at the start of every sentence? Have you used a variety of sentence structures?
   c. Leave one blank line and then use your plan to write the second paragraph, repeating the same checks.
   d. Do this for paragraphs three and four, remembering to leave a blank line between each paragraph.
   e. Re-read your last sentence. Does it bring the writing to a good end? How could you improve it?

8 Creative and imaginative writing

Writing

Assessment objective

- Organise information and ideas, using structural and grammatical features to support coherence and cohesion of texts (AO5)
- Communicate clearly, effectively and imaginatively, selecting and adapting tone, style and register for different forms, purposes and audiences (AO5)

Assessment links

English Language Paper 1 question 6

English term

*__Connotation:__ An idea, feeling or impression that a word or phrase creates in the reader's mind

Texts

The longer extract for analysis in this unit should be downloaded and printed from the Active Teach Library (see page v) so that it can be read in full and annotated.

8.1 In the frame: using pictures to write creatively

You will always be given the opportunity to write about a picture in your GCSE English exam. It can be a good option to choose because you are instantly presented with some ideas you can develop in your writing.

Take a few minutes to look at the picture before you begin writing. The examiner will be looking to see how imaginative you are in responding to the picture. They will want you to write powerfully, tapping into the mood or atmosphere suggested by the picture. You will need to express the connotations* the picture conjures up in your mind. Connotation is crucial to the impact your writing will have on the reader.

Activity 1

Look carefully at the painting *Flanders* by the German artist Otto Dix. The painting shows a battlefield scene from the First World War.

1. Use the checklist on the left to decide what is suggested by the people, objects, setting and colours in the painting.

Checklist

People

- their posture (the way they are standing or sitting)
- the expressions on their faces
- the clothes they are wearing

Objects – what has the artist included in the painting?

The setting

- where they are sitting
- the time of day
- the weather

Colour – the main colours used

Connotation – What ideas or feelings might the artist want to create in the viewer? What mood is suggested? What effect might the painting have on the viewer?

8.1 In the frame: using pictures to write creatively

2. In pairs, discuss your responses to the painting.

   a. Were any of your responses to the first task similar?

   b. Were any of your responses to the first task different?

   c. List five adjectives that you both agree describe the mood or atmosphere of the painting.

3. On your own, write a 75-word paragraph describing the painting. Make sure your writing captures a strong sense of the mood or atmosphere you sensed in the painting.

4. Swap your work with a partner. Make one change to your partner's work to make the writing even more powerful. You could change a single word, or alter the punctuation to lengthen or shorten a sentence. Give a reason for your change.

Activity 2

In the exam you will be given a choice of two pictures; the first thing you need to do is decide which picture stimulates your imagination more.

Look at the two images below.

1. Choose **one** of the images in order to **write about being lonely**.

2. Spend two to three minutes noting down the things that strike you in the image you have chosen. Consider all of the points in the checklist in Activity 1.

3. Use a four- or five-paragraph grid to plan what you are going to write and where. See Unit 7 mini assessment, page 97 for an example of this.

4. Write your response, checking each paragraph against your plan as you go.

5. Swap your work with a partner. Give feedback on three strengths of the piece and three ideas that would help to improve it.

Examiner tip
Look back at the suggestions for how to plan your work in Unit 7.6.

Examiner tip
When writing about pictures in the exam, remember that the image can be interpreted in a broad number of ways.

8 Creative and imaginative writing

8.2 Creating tension: it's all got very tense – Part 1

Horror films, crime fiction, TV thrillers: we love being on the edge of our seat, watching and reading exciting things. Why do we get tense as dramas build up? It is because we are given clues and indications that something – we do not necessarily know what – is about to happen. Writers use a variety of techniques to create tension and build drama. You can also use these in your writing.

> **Examiner tip**
>
> Remember to focus your writing on information and ideas appropriate for your audience and the exam conditions. Extreme or uncontrolled violence is not likely to be rewarded positively in the exam.

Activity 3

Look at the image below.

1. What do you think is going to happen next?
2. What clues in the picture helped you to make that decision?

8.2 Creating tension: it's all got very tense – Part 2

Extract from *The Woman in White* by Wilkie Collins

Read this extract. The narrator is walking back to London alone late at night. He has arrived at a deserted crossroads.

In one moment, every drop of blood in my body was brought to a stop by the touch of a hand laid lightly and suddenly on my shoulder from behind me.

I turned on the instant, with my fingers tightening round the handle of my stick.

There, in the middle of the broad bright high-road – there, as if it had that moment sprung out of the earth or dropped from the heaven – stood the figure of a solitary woman, dressed from head to foot in white garments, her face bent in grave inquiry on mine, her hand pointing to the dark cloud over London, as I faced her.

I was far too seriously startled by the suddenness with which this extraordinary apparition* stood before me, in the dead of night and in that lonely place, to ask what she wanted. The strange woman spoke first.

'Is that the road to London?' she said.

I looked attentively at her, as she put that singular question to me. It was then nearly one o'clock. All I could discern* distinctly by the moonlight was a colourless, youthful face, meagre* and sharp to look at about the cheeks and chin; large, grave, wistfully attentive eyes; nervous, uncertain lips; and light hair of a pale, brownish-yellow hue. There was nothing wild, nothing immodest* in her manner: it was quiet and self-controlled, a little melancholy* and a little touched by suspicion; not exactly the manner of a lady, and, at the same time, not the manner of a woman in the humblest rank of life. The voice, little as I had yet heard of it, had something curiously still and mechanical in its tones, and the utterance was remarkably rapid. She held a small bag in her hand: and her dress – bonnet, shawl, and gown all of white – was, so far as I could guess, certainly not composed of very delicate or very expensive materials. Her figure was slight, and rather above the average height – her gait* and actions free from the slightest approach to extravagance. This was all that I could observe of her in the dim light and under the perplexingly strange circumstances of our meeting. What sort of a woman she was, and how she came to be out alone in the high-road, an hour after midnight, I altogether failed to guess. The one thing of which I felt certain was that the grossest of mankind could not have misconstrued* her motive in speaking, even at that suspiciously late hour and in that suspiciously lonely place.

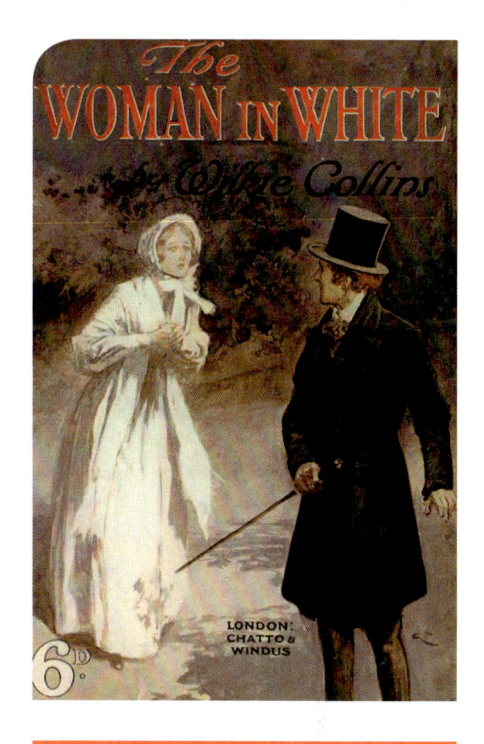

Glossary

*Apparition:** A ghost or spirit

*Discern:** To work something out

*Meagre:** Thin, skeletal

*Immodest:** Improper

*Melancholy:** Sad

*Gait:** The way a person walks

*Misconstrued:** Misunderstood

8 Creative and imaginative writing

It takes a lot of preparation to make a film. Although you may only see speaking and action in the final film, a lot of writing has gone on beforehand, in particular, in the creation of the storyboard.

Activity 4

Imagine you have been commissioned by a film company to write the storyboard for the extract from *The Woman in White* on page 101. The film company want to see if you are imaginative enough to write the screenplay for the whole film, although you are only concentrating on the extract for this task.

> **Examiner tip**
>
> Camera angles are also covered in Unit 3. See page 42.

1. In pairs, create a storyboard for the scene from *The Woman in White* on page 101. Use the template below as a guide.

SHOT SUMMARY Brief notes on what the shot will show	VISUAL Sketch what will appear on the screen	SHOT DESCRIPTION • Type of shot (for example, long shot, close-up) • Camera angle • Lighting ideas	AUDIO Music Sound Effects Dialogue
Shot 1			
Shot 2			
Shot 3			

2. Compare your completed storyboard with one created by another pair. What similarities are there between the two approaches? What did you do differently?

3. Which sections of each storyboard do you think are most successful, and why?

8.2 Creating tension: it's all got very tense – Part 2

Activity 5

1. Think about what you learned when transforming the extract from *The Woman in White* from page to screen. Did you find the process difficult?

2. With a partner, discuss what you notice about the techniques the author, Wilkie Collins, uses to build up the drama and suspense. Think about:

People: How are they described? How are they dressed? What attitudes do they have to each other?

Events: What happens? How do the characters react? Why are things presented in the order they are? How does the writer want us to react?

Setting: What kind of place has Collins chosen? What feelings does it conjure up? What details stick out?

Tone: What is the feeling created by the writer? What things are important in establishing this tone?

> **Examiner tip**
>
> You can use the examples in the table in Unit 7, on page 88 to help you describe the tone established.

Activity 6

1. You are going to use one of the scenarios below to write your own dramatic narrative.

   a. **Lost on the moor:** You have been walking for two hours when a thick fog comes down. You do not know which direction to take to reach home. You hear a ghostly barking sound nearby…

   b. **Alone in a strange house:** You are staying in a holiday house. Everyone else has gone out to do some shopping. Two hours pass. It gets dark. You hear what you think are floorboards creaking upstairs…

2. Plan your writing before you start. Look back at Unit 7.6, on page 96 for more guidance on planning. Aim to use approximately the same number of words as the Collins extract – about 400. This is usually about one page of handwriting. The mistake many students make in the exam is trying to write a whole novel in 400 words. Instead, concentrate on one part of the story. In the extract you read, Collins developed just one incident. In your writing, you should plan to do the same.

3. Start your narrative by establishing who you are, where you are, and why you are there. This can be done in the first few sentences of the opening paragraph.

4. Use the rest of your piece of writing to develop the one incident described in the title.

8 Creative and imaginative writing

> **Examiner tip**
> In the exam, make sure your plan includes details about the setting as well as the events.

8.3 On location: creating a setting

Setting the scene

Finding the right location is very important. For filmmakers, for example, locations can help to sell a film, as well as being a big part of the overall 'look' of a film. Filmmakers have the great advantage of being able to establish the location where action will take place in a matter of seconds with a well composed shot.

If you are a writer, you will need to give your reader a sense of where events are happening – this is the **setting** of a piece of writing. The big advantage for writers is that they do not have to move out of their seats to find their settings. All they have to do is picture the setting in their head and start writing!

Activity 7

1. Write four or five sentences that describe your bedroom. Try to bring out unusual little details which make it a personal space and which will give your reader an idea of how you feel about the room.

2. Exchange your work with a partner. Give feedback on your partner's answers, listing three things that best helped you to understand how the writer feels about their room.

Activity 8

> **Glossary**
> *Location scout: A person who finds the right locations for filming movies or television programmes

Imagine you are a location scout* and you have been asked to find locations for a new crime series. You had taken some photographs to take back to the office, but your camera has broken. The producer of the show needs to make a decision about locations quickly, so she asks you to send her a description of the two main locations you are recommending. The photographs you took of these locations are shown in the images on this page. They are labelled Location A and Location B.

1. Write a 100-word description of each location. Use the points below to help you.

   - Make sure you give a clear description of each place so that the producer has a good idea of what it looks like.
   - Add in some details about the feelings inspired by each location. What is it that would make them suitable locations for a crime drama?

2. Swap your writing with a partner. Which details have each of you chosen to describe? Did you have similar views about the feel of the places?

Location A

Location B

8.3 On location: creating a setting

Describing a setting

When describing a setting, you need to focus on people, buildings, nature, vehicles: any physical features that will help to build an image in the reader's head. But you will also want the setting to create a mood or tone to complement where the action is happening.

Extract from *The Tobacconist* by Robert Seethaler

Read the description below from the novel *The Tobacconist* by Robert Seethaler. The extract describes a fisherman's cottage where the character Franz Huchel lives with his mother.

> The weather shook the hut on every side. The beams groaned, the shutters banged outside, and the wooden roof shingles, thickly overgrown with moss, flapped in the storm. Rain pelted against windowpanes, driven by gusts of wind, and on the sills a few decapitated geraniums drowned in their tubs. The iron Jesus on the wall above the old clothes box wobbled as if at any moment he might tear himself from his nails and leap down from the cross and from the shore of the nearby lake came the crash of fishing boats slammed against their moorings by the pounding waves.

In just 100 words, Seethaler has set the scene with a clear picture of the cottage, using the description to provide the reader with information.

- We know it is a small building because he calls it a 'hut'.
- It is near a lake on which there are fishing boats.
- It is probably old: the shingles (wooden tiles) are 'overgrown with moss'.
- It has shutters on the windows and geraniums on the window sills.

Seethaler uses his description to create a very dark mood. Personification is used: for example, geranium plants are described as having been 'decapitated' and 'drowned in their tubs'. The violent mood is created by Seethaler's choice of verbs: 'banged'; 'pelted'; 'drowned'; 'tear'; 'slammed'. Most startling of all is the description of Jesus, who is about to 'tear himself from his nails and leap down from the cross'.

Activity 9

Write the opening paragraph you might use to start an exam response to each of the following ideas:

- a frightening experience you have had
- a memorable visit to a place of interest to you.

Remember to set the scene with a vivid description of the setting and mood.

> **Examiner tip**
>
> Your Paper 1 GCSE writing task will ask you to write about a real or imagined experience. It is a very good idea to start with a description of the setting.

8 Creative and imaginative writing

> **English terms**
>
> ***Autobiography:** Writing about yourself, usually your life story; a period of time in your life or a specific experience you have had

8.4 Autobiography: all about you

It is often said that each of us has a novel inside waiting to be written. It has also been said that every first novel is a thinly-veiled autobiography*. This is because, when it comes to writing about ourselves, we are the world's number one expert and it is easier to write about what we know well.

The writing question on Paper 1 Imaginative Writing often asks you to write about a personal experience. Writing about yourself is called autobiography. It is always written in the first person and the theme of the writing is always some aspect of the author's life.

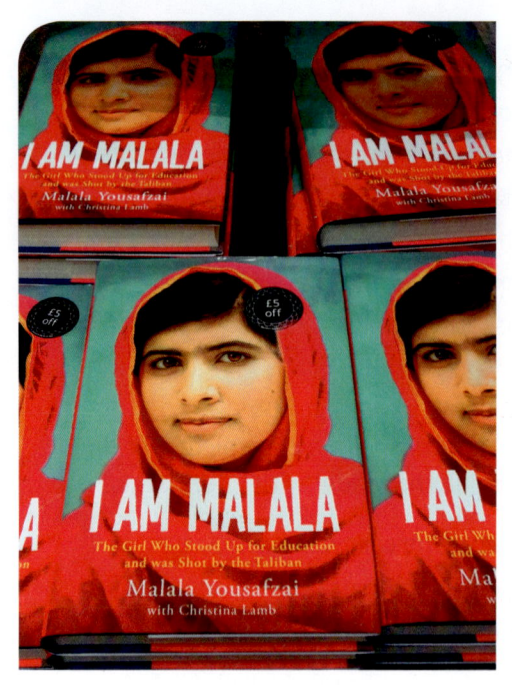

The Paper 1 writing questions may be phrased like this:

> 'Write about a time when something unusual happened to you.'

You could think of something that has actually happened in your life and base your writing on that experience, as this student did.

> It was a Sunday and my friend, Meg, and I were going for a walk with my dog, Skipper. Suddenly, right in front of us, a car mounted the pavement and went into the wall of a house. We approached it to see if anyone was hurt. Inside was a man but he was okay, apart from a cut on his forehead. We used Meg's phone to call the police and tell them what had happened. They arrived quite quickly and thanked us for phoning them.

The spelling and punctuation are correct in this student answer, and the response does deal with a topic relevant to the question. However, there's nothing particularly exciting about this piece of writing, either.

8.4 Autobiography: all about you

One strength of the student's answer is that it focuses on just one incident. This is important as a piece of writing that tries to tell the reader about too many things often does not go into enough descriptive detail and may turn into a long uninteresting list.

Activity 10

Rewrite the student's opening, but make it more interesting by focusing on two of the key choices any writer has to make: words and sentence structure.

1. Change the three verbs which have been underlined for you in the student's answer.

2. Alter some of the sentence structure, using one or two very short sentences to create impact.

3. Rewrite the opening sentence so it grabs the reader's attention and makes them want to keep reading.

4. Swap your writing with a partner. Tell each other whether you think your changes have improved the student's response.

Artistic licence

When a writer 'stretches the truth' by making an event more interesting or dramatic than it was it is called using 'artistic licence'. When you are writing about something that has happened to you it does not all have to be true – it could be completely made up. Although an autobiography is supposed to be about your life, the writing you do in response to a question like the one on page 106 is marked on how imaginative it is, not how truthful it is. You can exaggerate events, add extra events or information to the original event or change the people who were involved. No-one will ever know but you.

Activity 11

Another problem with the student's opening paragraph is that it tells the whole story in five sentences. It has a beginning, a middle and an end, but no development of the ideas. It is more like a *plan* for the writing, with each sentence being a topic for a paragraph.

Rewrite the following sentences from the student answer:

> We approached it to see if anyone was hurt. Inside was a man but he was okay, apart from a cut on his forehead.

Do this by:

1. Writing a description of the wreckage of the vehicle, building a picture for the reader of the damage to the car.

2. Changing the description of the man inside the car. Tell the reader more about how he was and about his injuries.

8 Creative and imaginative writing

8.5 Developing a tone of voice: it's all in the tone

One way to make your writing stand out is to develop a distinctive tone of voice, as has already been looked at in Unit 7.3. This is important when writing about yourself and your own life, as the choice of tone will help to make your writing more personal and individual.

Formal or **informal**	**Humorous** or **serious**	**Polite** restrained measured	**Upset** hurt, pained
Scary afraid, alarmed	**Bored** apathetic weary	**Confused** baffled puzzled	**Sarcastic** cynical, provocative
Dejected gloomy, miserable	**Annoyed** cross exasperated	**Angry** enraged fuming furious	**Dramatic** melodramatic, over-the-top
Cheerful jovial, light-hearted	**Tense** agitated, uneasy	**Enthusiastic** passionate, eager	**Shocked** staggered, stunned

In the exam, you should focus on using a wide vocabulary and make sure you punctuate both accurately and imaginatively. You might be able to use one or two slang expressions for effect, if you choose, but it must be clear that this is intentional. For example, if you are using dialogue, this could be the place to capture the speaker's character by using slang.

Point of view

At the beginning of this unit, it was said that you are the biggest expert on yourself. But other people do not always see you as you might see yourself. The Italian playwright, Luigi Pirandello, felt there could be lots of different views of 'you':

> 'This is the real drama for me; the belief that we all [...] think of ourselves as one single person: but it's not true: each of us is several different people, and all these people live inside us. With one person we seem like this and with another we seem very different. But we always have the illusion of being the same person for everybody and of always being the same person in everything we do. But it's not true! It's not true!'

Activity 12

You are going to write about one of the many versions of you, as described by Pirandello.

1. Choose a person who you think knows you very well. Imagine how they might describe you and make some notes.

2. Plan, and then write, a description of yourself, but as you think that person sees you. Write around 400 words. Remember to write the piece with a very distinctive tone of voice. You can make it amusing, sarcastic, critical or a mixture of all of those things, and more. Whatever you do, do not just write a list of characteristics.

Mini Assessment

The skills you have developed in this unit focus on communicating clearly, effectively and imaginatively, using a variety of different methods, including using a range of vocabulary and sentence structure, and accurate spelling and punctuation.

The assessments on this page will allow you to test your writing skills and review your progress in preparation for exam-focused work.

Paper 1 Section B Writing: responding to an image

Look carefully at the picture on the right. Then answer the questions that follow.

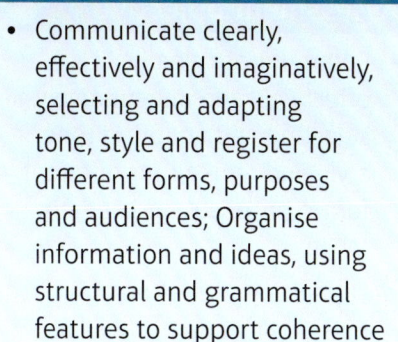

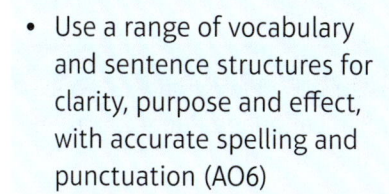

1. Consider the picture as the basis for a piece of imaginative writing in response to the question:

   Write about a time when you, or someone you know, received an important message. Your response could be real or imagined.

2. Write a list of points of focus in the picture to support your creation of setting. Think about:
   - objects
   - the room
   - colour
   - connotations of the picture.

3. Jot down a list of three or four possible ideas for your writing. You might discuss them with a partner to see which ones would enable you to:
   - plan a series of paragraphs that you could complete within 30 minutes
   - engage your reader
   - draw on people and events that you know something about.

   Tick the idea you decide to use.

4. Write an engaging opening paragraph drawing on what you have learned in this chapter and your ideas for setting from task 2.

5. Check your work for:
   - relevance to the focus of the question
   - clear presentation of setting, voice, point of view and character(s)
   - variety of sentence structures
   - accurate spelling, punctuation and grammar.

> **Assessment objective**
> - Communicate clearly, effectively and imaginatively, selecting and adapting tone, style and register for different forms, purposes and audiences; Organise information and ideas, using structural and grammatical features to support coherence and cohesion of texts (AO5)
> - Use a range of vocabulary and sentence structures for clarity, purpose and effect, with accurate spelling and punctuation (AO6)

Skill	🟢🟠🔴
I can interpret an image, identifying key elements of objective, setting, colour and connotation.	
I can use an image and question to inspire writing.	
I can select appropriate ideas to engage the reader.	
I can use appropriate techniques to begin a piece of creative writing, e.g. vocabulary, variety of sentence structures and language techniques.	
I can use a voice that makes the piece interesting and believable to the reader.	

9 Transactional writing

Writing

Assessment objective

- Communicate clearly, effectively and imaginatively, selecting and adapting tone, style and register for different forms, purposes and audiences (AO5)
- Organise information and ideas, using structural and grammatical features (AO5)

Assessment links

English Language Paper 2, question 8 or 9

9.1 Writing a speech: get it off your chest – Part 1

In the English Language Paper 2, you may be asked to write a speech.

When you hear somebody giving a really good speech, you might forget that it is not spontaneous. Most great speeches are carefully written so that the intended meaning is clear, and the message is delivered in an engaging way.

We will all probably have to give a speech of some sort in our lives, perhaps at school, for a job interview or at a wedding, so it is not just a GCSE skill you are developing when you learn how to write a good speech – it is a skill for life.

Only 10 per cent of our communication is done by writing things down; over 90 per cent is done by speaking. Employers often rate an employee's ability to speak clearly and communicate effectively through speech as highly as they rate accurate writing.

It may seem a bit odd to have a writing task about something that will ultimately be spoken (i.e. the speech will be read out) but almost all formal speeches have been scripted in advance. This is because there are very few people who can make a speech without some preparation. Most of us need to plan carefully, thinking ahead about what we are going to say.

Activity 1

1. Working with a partner, read through Mohammed's draft speech on the following page and discuss how successful you think he has been in making his point. Think about:
   - how persuasive the speech is
   - whether Mohammed achieved his purpose
   - three things you think might improve his speech.

2. Look at the section 'Speech writing techniques' on page 112 and the list of the rhetorical devices* in the table. Which devices does Mohammed use in his speech?

English term

*Rhetorical device: A technique used in writing or speaking to influence or persuade the audience

9.1 Writing a speech: get it off your chest – Part 1

Social Media: a bad habit?

In my opinion, I think going on social media all the time is a bad habit. It's becoming very common these days for children to be spending hours and hours looking at their phones or computers for this stuff. That's over a whole day a week! Why are they doing this? Is it just because they see all their friends doing it and they don't want to feel left out? Or is it really that they actually enjoy it? Why is this happening? Is it all about having as many friends as you can? But do they know the consequences of spending all those hours on social media? Who's checking this out? Nobody. I know this girl, she was so stressed out by not having about a thousand likes for everything she posted that she nearly made herself ill. What is going on? Are we really only as good as the number of times someone, somewhere, who we probably don't even know, says they like us? And loads of people get bullied on these social media sites. People can hide behind the fact that they can say whatever they like and not have to face the consequences. Some people are saying that our generation is losing the skill of actually talking to each other face-to-face because we would rather just go home and put up a post instead. And a lot of it isn't true anyway, like people saying they have been to Florida and Disneyland for their holiday when they have really only been to Butlins Minehead. It's time for the posting to stop. Schools need to teach young people that there is more to life than spending all your time staring at a screen. It needs to stop and it needs to stop today.

Activity 2

Read Mohammed's speech from Activity 1 again.

1. Break the speech up into paragraphs, ensuring each paragraph has a clear topic. *(cut up photocopy + glue in)*

2. Try to add any of the rhetorical devices on page 112 that Mohammed has not used. Use a different one in each paragraph. *pick 2 rhetorical devices and add to the speech*

Examiner tip

Sometimes students overuse certain features in their writing – for example, rhetorical questions – and this can take away from their impact on the audience. Always check your writing to make sure it is achieving your intended effect. The quality not the quantity of the features and techniques you use is more important.

9 Transactional writing

9.2 Writing a speech: get it off your chest – Part 2

Speech writing techniques

There are a number of techniques that speech writers can use to try to engage an audience. We call these rhetorical devices.

Rhetorical device	Purpose	Example
Facts and statistics	To prove what you are saying	Sixty-six per cent of the people interviewed thought fox hunting should be banned.
Personal pronouns Words such as: I, you, us, we, ours	Makes the reader/listener feel they are being personally spoken to	I feel very strongly that the time has come to act. If we act together, we can do something about this.
Different sentence lengths	Adds variety and creates impact	(Short sentence) Things must change.
Emotive language Emotional words or phrases	To move or shock the reader/listener	Chickens are kept in appalling conditions, with no room to move or light to see, just so we can have cheap food.
Imperative sentence One that includes a verb	Persuades the reader/listener to take action	Call now!
Rhetorical question Asking a question but without providing/expecting an answer	Invites the reader/listener to think about their view on something	Why have we allowed this to happen in our country?
Personal anecdote An example of your own experience	Adds personal insight to something	My own father was one of those who suffered from the poor care.
Flattery Complimenting the reader/listener	Makes the reader/listener feel good about themselves	Of course, you are not the sort of person who would do such awful things.
Triples To say something three times, often slightly differently each time	Reinforces/emphasises a point or argument	This sort of discrimination is unacceptable, immoral and uncivilised.

Examiner tip

Triples are discussed in more detail on pages 90–91.

9.2 Writing a speech: get it off your chest – Part 2

✱ Activity 3

45mins

Write a speech to try to persuade people to do one of the following:

- donate money to a charity of your choice
- join an organisation
- give something up.

Your speech should last about three minutes. This will mean writing about 500 words.

1. Write down all of the things you think might help to persuade your audience to do what you are suggesting. Don't worry about writing in full sentences yet – this is just a rough list. Include as many ideas as you possibly can – you will cut the list down later.

2. Think carefully about which of the ideas on your list will be the most persuasive. You should select about four or five 'big ideas'.

3. Using a paragraph for each of the big ideas you have selected, write a draft of your speech. Getting the ideas to flow is the most important thing at this stage. You can fine tune your writing later.

4. Check your work to see if you have used some of the rhetorical devices you have learned about. Could you add any to your speech to give it greater impact?

5. Proofread your speech, checking that your punctuation and spelling are accurate.

Activity 4

How a speech is delivered to an audience is important. The tasks below will help you to prepare to deliver your speech. Remember, though, that you will not have to read out your speech in the exam.

1. Work with a partner and take it in turns to read your speeches to each other. As you listen to your partner's speech, make notes about how well they are using the following non-verbal skills:

    - intonation*
    - facial expressions
    - eye contact
    - volume
    - pace
    - emphasis*.

2. Practise delivering your speech on your own. Try to reach a stage where you do not have to look down at the script the whole time and can make eye contact with the audience.

3. If possible, record or film yourself giving your speech, perhaps to some other students in your class.

> **Examiner tip**
> When crafting your writing, always think about the impact of your work choices and keep your audience in mind.

> **English terms**
> ***Intonation:** The rise and fall of the voice when speaking
>
> ***Emphasis:** Stress given to a word when speaking

> **Examiner tip**
> The work you have completed in this unit can be used to support your work in Spoken Language. This skill is very highly prized by employers. Getting a Distinction for Spoken Language could mark you out from the crowd at any future interviews for college or jobs.

9 Transactional writing

> **Examiner tip**
> Always remember what your reader needs to know and understand.

> **Examiner tip**
> Remember 'TAPS': text type, audience, purpose, source. (See page 77.)

> **English terms**
> ***Formal language:** A less personal style of language – more commonly used when writing
>
> ***Informal language:** A more personal style of language – more commonly used when speaking

9.3 Writing a letter: to whom it may concern

Letter-writing decisions

In the examination task for Paper 2, questions 8 and 9, you will sometimes be asked to write a letter. Some common letters you may be asked to write are:

- advising someone of your view on a particular topic
- complaining about an injustice
- persuading someone to do something
- applying for a job.

The purpose of the letter will be made very clear in the task. The first thing you need to decide is whether you will be writing in formal language* or informal language*.

The letter you will be asked to write will usually require formal language as this is the language you use:

- when communicating with someone you do not know very well
- in 'official' situations, such as when applying for a job.

Unless the letter you are asked to write is to a friend or close relative, informal language will be inappropriate.

Activity 5

You are going to write a letter to your local Member of Parliament about a plan to knock down your home to make way for a new road.

1. With a partner, write the opening few sentences of your letter. First, decide on the tone, using one of the suggestions in Box A. Remember that first impressions count, so you will want to engage the reader of your letter quickly and effectively. Make sure your opening paragraph makes an impact.

   Box A

angry	shocked
enraged	dejected

2. Write the opening to your letter again, but this time use one of the tones in Box B.

   Box B

cheerful	polite
humorous	sarcastic

3. How has changing the tone affected the impact of your letter? Which do you think would be more effective, and why?

9.3 Writing a letter: to whom it may concern

Letter from Mahatma Gandhi to Adolf Hitler

On the right is a letter from the Indian pacifist leader Mahatma Gandhi to Adolf Hitler. He is asking Hitler to stop actions that could cause a world war.

Activity 6

Read the letter from Mahatma Gandhi to Adolf Hitler.

1. How would you describe the tone of the letter? You can choose from the words below to help you.

   exasperated   gloomy   agitated   friendly   reasonable

   calm   sarcastic   polite   passionate   measured

2. Would you say more than one tone is being used?

3. Which words or phrases from the letter would you select as evidence for your views?

Activity 7

Write a formal letter using the appropriate greeting.

1. Choose one of the options from the list below, then plan and write a draft of your letter:
   - write to the editor of a fashion magazine complaining about the ultra-thin models used in their advertisements
   - write to the managing director of a cosmetics company urging them to stop testing their products on animals
   - write to the local council complaining about the lack of sports facilities in your area
   - write to your local Member of Parliament to persuade them that young people of 16 should be allowed to vote.

2. Swap your draft with a partner and ask them to comment on:
   - **purpose** – does your letter make your opinion on the topic clear?
   - the **ideas** you have used in your letter – will the reader be engaged? Have you used facts to back up your points? Are there personal anecdotes to add interest to the letter?
   - **organisation** – does the letter start powerfully, introduce your main idea, develop it and end by reinforcing your point of view?
   - the **accuracy** of your punctuation and spelling.

3. Edit your draft letter, thinking about the four points your partner used to respond to your work.

4. Look at the final version of your letter carefully to check all the punctuation and spelling is accurate.

DEAR FRIEND,

Friends have been urging me to write to you for the sake of humanity. But I have resisted their request, because of the feeling that any letter from me would be an impertinence. Something tells me that I must not calculate and that I must make my appeal for whatever it may be worth.

It is quite clear that you are today the one person in the world who can prevent a war which may reduce humanity to a savage state. Must you pay that price for an object however worthy it may appear to you to be? Will you listen to the appeal of one who has deliberately shunned the method of war not without considerable success? Anyway I anticipate your forgiveness, if I have erred in writing to you.

I remain,
Your sincere friend,
M. K. Gandhi

Examiner tip

If you do not know the name of the person you are writing to, you should begin *Dear Sir/Madam* and end *Yours faithfully*. If you know their name, begin *Dear Ms. Sutcliffe*, for example, and end *Yours sincerely*. In the exam you do not need to include addresses and dates.

9 Transactional writing

9.4 Expressing your view: a view from your side

The English Language Paper 2 writing questions will sometimes ask you to write a piece for a newspaper to express your view about an issue. The task may be phrased in a way similar to the exam-style question below.

Your piece of writing will need to be both informative and entertaining, using carefully chosen words and structure. Your choice of tone is also important. When reporting serious news, journalists usually use a formal tone, but for features or opinion pieces the tone does not have to be as formal. These can be more like magazine articles.

Extract from 'Britain's worst kept guilty secret: We can't get enough of fast food' by Stuart Maconie

Read the extract below from the *Daily Mirror* in which columnist Stuart Maconie is exploring the British obsession with fast food.

Britain's worst kept guilty secret: We can't get enough of fast food

Stuart Maconie, *Daily Mirror*

We British have always been a busy people. We have things to do, people to see, small countries to colonise, wars to fight, scandals to revel in.

Not for us the long, lazy, lunches of the indolent French and Italians with their cruel hamster patés and effeminate 'wine'.

No, we have always needed something hot, tasty and nutritionally valueless to eat al fresco as we enjoy a public hanging, bear-baiting contest, or the burning of some poor sap who backed the wrong king. Nowadays, it's a football match or a fight at the taxi rank, but it's the same thing.

For us Brits, it hasn't been a decent Friday night unless we have witnessed some act of violence with chilli sauce and chip fat running down our chin.

Of course, not all 'fast food' is this kind of nocturnal fighting fuel variety.

There's a long and rich tradition of ethnically diverse, artery-clogging snack food that's been guiltily enjoyed by Britons.

Statistics suggest that while sales of garage forecourt pork pies are increasing, the number of people who say they eat them is dwindling.

So it's official. We are a nation of furtive fast foodies, secret scoffers.

9.4 Expressing your view: a view from

Activity 8

1. Discuss with a partner how the writing in the *Daily Mirror* extract is different from sections of a newspaper which report on current events.

2. Which of the words in the table below do you think best describes the tone of the extract? You may select more than one, but you must identify examples from the extract to back up your choices.

informal	humorous	polite	upset
cynical	provocative	ironic	sarcastic
passionate	jovial	light-hearted	over-the-top

One feature of Maconie's writing, which is the same as other tabloid newspaper* writing, is the use of very short paragraphs. In fact, most of them are only one sentence long. This moves the reader along and makes it easier to take in the article quickly. Tabloid newspapers like the *Daily Mirror* and *The Sun* are designed to be a quick read.

Activity 9

Imagine you are a journalist for one of the broadsheet newspapers* like *The Times* or *The Guardian*. You are going to write a short opinion piece about the state of education in the African country Mali, comparing it with schooling in the UK.

1. Carefully study the three photographs on page 118, which will be printed with your article. Each photo provides a topic for one paragraph, but you must choose the order in which to use them.

2. Make some notes on what you think are the important differences between this school in Mali and a typical school in the UK. These are the main points you will cover in your writing.

3. Use other sources, as well as the photos provided on the next page, to gather information for your article. These could be websites, newspapers or textbooks.

u> use internet to research for 10-15mins.

> **Examiner tip**
> Remember to use paragraphs. Occasionally you might want to use one- or two-sentence paragraphs for effect.

> **English terms**
> *****Tabloid newspaper:** A newspaper that reports current events but also focuses on popular stories, for example, about celebrities
>
> *****Broadsheet newspaper:** A newspaper that focuses more on serious news stories with a greater focus on good reporting and writing

transactional writing

A. In the classroom

B. Playing

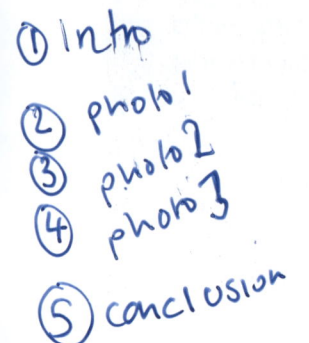

C. School building

Handwritten notes:
1. Intro
2. photo 1
3. photo 2
4. photo 3
5. conclusion

4. Plan your piece of writing.

5. Decide on the tone you are going to use. You can use the table below to help you.

| formal/informal | serious | measured | passionate |
| humorous | balanced | angry | provocative |

6. Draft a short introductory paragraph, followed by three topic paragraphs based on the photographs.

7. Draft a short final paragraph, clearly setting out your view about the differences.

8. Finally, review and edit your article. You should think about the following:

- Content: will your readers be engaged by what you have said?
- Tone: have you established a strong voice that conveys your opinion?
- Organisation: is each paragraph well-constructed with an introduction, development and conclusion?
- Accuracy: is your spelling, punctuation and grammar correct?

9.5 Persuasive writing: give us your money!

Every day we are bombarded by advertising trying to get us to part with our money. Persuasion is big business, and at its heart are very careful choices of words and pictures.

Activity 10

Look at the two images below.

1. With a partner, discuss where you might expect to see each image used – in what type of advertisement? What do you think each image could be trying to get you to do? Try to think of more than one option for each image. Make notes about the clues in the pictures that influenced your decisions.

2. Compare your ideas with those of another pair of students.

3. Working with your original partner, write a one-sentence caption for each image that you think could be used to reinforce the message it is trying to convey. Think carefully about your word choice.

The first image was used on a donation bag asking for donations of old clothes. Donation bags are pushed through people's letter boxes. The other is hoping to attract new donations to its charitable cause. Although the purposes are slightly different, both of them use an emotional appeal which charities hope will make people donate.

9 Transactional writing

Activity 11

The paragraphs below are all taken from a leaflet used by the charity *Crisis* in their 2017 Christmas appeal. They have been jumbled up.

1. How would you order these paragraphs to most effectively persuade people to pay £26.08 to help a homeless person at Christmas?

   A For us, Christmas is crucial. Your gift now could be the start of getting someone off the streets and out of homelessness for good. It could even save their life.

   B These days, £26.08 won't get you much. But if you use it to reserve a place at this year's *Crisis at Christmas*, it will give someone who is homeless more than you can imagine.

   C Did you know that the average age of death for a homeless person is just 47? It doesn't bear thinking about.

   D *Crisis* is the national charity for homeless people. No one should be homeless, and we are committed to ending homelessness once and for all.

   E Being homeless at Christmas can be hell. There's nowhere that's safe, nowhere that's yours – nowhere to go out from or come back to. It can be impossible to find enough to eat and to look after yourself. And when the bitter cold and pelting rain kick in, you really feel it.

   F Please can you give £26.08 to reserve a place for someone who's homeless at *Crisis at Christmas*?

   G Dear Friend,

   H People can treat you like dirt too. Some people think it's a laugh to abuse you, just because you are homeless – and you can't get away. While the shops and pubs welcome people in, you're stuck alone on the outside.

2. Which of the paragraphs do you think uses the most emotional tone to persuade? How does it do this?

3. Look at your answer to task 2. Was this the paragraph you found most effective when you ordered them in task 1? If not, why not?

9.5 Persuasive writing: give us your money!

Activity 12

1. Look at the three images below, labelled 1, 2 and 3. Choose words from the table below that you think best describe each image.

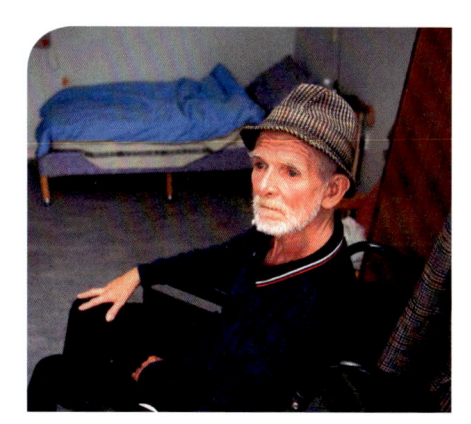

Image 1

Image 2

Image 3

lonely	pathetic	aggressive	friendly	desperate
confident	untidy	devious	downcast	dejected
sad	pessimistic	depressed	disheartened	hostile

2. Choose the image you think would be most effective in persuading people to give money to *Crisis*.

3. Write your own strapline* to introduce the content of the *Crisis* appeal that you read in Activity 11.

Writing a leaflet

The writing questions on the GCSE English Language Paper 2 may ask you to write a leaflet for a given purpose. You will not, of course, have to include pictures. But you should see your first sentence as doing the same job as a picture: grabbing your reader's attention and making them want to read on.

Activity 13

1. Write straplines to catch the reader's attention for leaflets designed for the following purposes:

   - Persuading people to donate money to buy shelters for refugees fleeing a war zone.
   - Raising money for research into eating disorders such as anorexia and bulimia.
   - Stopping the use of racist language and chanting at football matches.

2. Share your ideas with a partner. Compare the word choices you have used. Which is the most emotive* word in each strapline? Can you suggest changes to each other's work which would give greater impact to the straplines?

English terms

*****Strapline:** A heading used in adverts. It is usually larger than the rest of the text, in a prominent position, and written to grab the reader's attention and make them read on

*****Emotive:** Something that is likely to cause an emotional response, for example, shock, upset

9 Transactional writing

If you write a leaflet for your writing task on Paper 2, remember the three choices you always have to make, whatever type of writing you are doing:

- choice of words
- choice of sentence structure
- how to organise your paragraphing.

The writers and designers of the *Crisis* leaflet faced the same choices. These choices are partly influenced by the **text type, audience** and **purpose** of the writing. In a leaflet, it is important to get the message across quickly and simply and also in a way that draws the reader in.

Word choice

You only have a small amount of time to grab your reader's attention, so word choice is very important. Words with an emotional impact will be an important part of the overall design. In the *Crisis* leaflet, instead of just saying, 'And when the cold and rain start….' the writer modifies each noun with a well-chosen adjective and adverb. The cold is not just cold, it is 'bitter'; the rain is 'pelting'; it doesn't just 'start' to rain, it 'kicks in'. We get a feeling of being attacked by the weather because of these word choices.

Sentences

Some short sentences are used to give impact to the message. For example, the strapline begins 'Just £26.08'. There is also a sentence with only five words: 'For us, Christmas is crucial'. None of the sentences in the leaflet are very long or complex because *Crisis* need the message to get through clearly and concisely. There are a variety of sentence lengths, though, and each one has been carefully thought through. For example, one of the longer sentences deliberately uses repetition for effect: 'There's nowhere that's safe, nowhere that's yours – nowhere to go out to or come home from'.

Paragraphs

Have you noticed that all of the paragraphs are very short? One paragraph has only one sentence, and three of the others have only two sentences. The longest has just four. This organisation of the information in the leaflet helps to move the reader through in small stages.

> **Examiner tip**
> TAPS is covered in more detail on page 77 of this book (Unit 6).

Activity 14

1. Choose one of the three leaflets from Activity 13, part 1.

2. Use the strapline you have already created and then write the rest of the leaflet. Use the *Crisis* leaflet as a model and aim for about seven or eight paragraphs. Remember to include at least two paragraphs that are four or five sentences long.

Mini Assessment

The skills you have developed in this unit focus on communicating clearly, effectively and imaginatively, using a variety of different methods, including using a range of vocabulary and sentence structure, and accurate spelling and punctuation.

The assessments on this page will allow you to test your writing skills and review your progress in preparation for exam-focused work.

Read the question below. Then answer the questions that follow.

> You have been asked to give a speech to parents at your school, to ask them to donate money for new sports facilities in your school. In your speech you could:
>
> - Suggest the ways sport will be developed in your school as a result of this money
> - Examine why it is important for students to be more involved in sport
> - Include any other ideas you have.

1. Identify the following aspects of the question above:
   - text type
   - audience
   - purpose

2. a. Write a list of at least six ideas that meet the first bullet point.

   'Suggest the ways sport will be developed in your school as a result of this money'

   b. Select three that you will use in your speech.

3. a. Write a list of at least six ideas that meet the second bullet point.

   'Examine why it is important for students to be more involved in sport'

   b. Select three that you will use in your speech.

4. Write down your plan of four or five topics or 'big ideas' to create a plan for your speech. Make sure each point links to the question. Use your answers to parts 1–3 above for support.

5. Write your speech, using your plan as your guide.

6. Check your work carefully.

Assessment objective

- Communicate clearly, effectively and imaginatively, selecting and adapting tone, style and register for different forms, purposes and audiences; Organise information and ideas, using structural and grammatical features to support coherence and cohesion of texts (AO5)
- Use a range of vocabulary and sentence structures for clarity, purpose and effect, with accurate spelling and punctuation (AO6)

Self-assessment

Look back at the work you have done in this unit. You can now review your performance on the skills you have practised.

Skill	🟢 🟠 🔴
I can write in the form that is set by the question	
I can write appropriately for a specific audience considering voice, tone and register	
I can select relevant ideas in line with the question set	
I can use appropriate rhetorical devices to engage the audience	
I can proofread my work to correct spelling, punctuation and grammar	

Preparing for your exams: Paper 1

Exam guidance

Exam technique: Paper 1 Fiction and Imaginative Writing

What is it worth?

Paper 1 is worth **40%** of your English Language GCSE.

There are two sections which are each worth 50% of the total marks for this paper:

Paper 1 Section A: Reading = 50%   Paper 1 Section B: Writing = 50%

What does it test?

Section A questions test three Reading Assessment Objectives:

AO1	• Identify and interpret explicit and implicit information and ideas • Select and synthesise evidence from different texts
AO2	Explain, comment on and analyse how writers use language and structure to achieve effects and influence readers, using relevant subject terminology to support their views
AO4	Evaluate texts critically and support this with appropriate textual references

Section B questions address two Writing Assessment Objectives:

AO5	• Communicate clearly, effectively and imaginatively, selecting and adapting tone, style and register for different forms, purposes and audiences. • Organise information and ideas, using structural and grammatical features to support coherence and cohesion of texts
AO6	Candidates must use a range of vocabulary and sentence structures for clarity, purpose and effect, with accurate spelling and punctuation

What does the paper contain?

Section A: Reading asks you to read and answer questions on **a 19th-century prose fiction extract**. It contains 4 questions.

- Question 1 (1 mark) asks you to identify explicit information (AO1)
- Question 2 (2 marks) asks you to identify explicit or implicit information (AO1)
- Question 3 (6 marks) asks you to focus on language and structure (AO2)
- Question 4 (15 marks) asks you to evaluate the extract in relation to a given focus (AO4)

> **Examiner tip**
> The text is around 650 words. Practise reading and understanding such extracts in 5 minutes.

Section B: Imaginative Writing asks you to choose one task from a choice of two: Question 5 **OR** Question 6 (AO5 and AO6). One question will offer a picture to respond to.

Your response can be real or imagined so you can draw on your imagination or base your writing on events that have happened to you, or to someone else.

Your reader should be 'general'.

You can write a narrative, a descriptive or a monologue. There should be clear organisation and structure with an opening, development of points and a conclusion.

What is the timing?

Paper 1 = one hour and 45 minutes in total.

- one hour on the Reading Section
- 45 minutes on the Writing Section

Reading	5 minutes reading time
	2 minutes per mark given to each question = 50 minutes
	5 minutes checking
Writing	45 minutes including planning and checking

Which techniques will help me to raise my grade?

This section of the textbook will outline techniques to help you do well. Activities focusing on each exam question type will be based on one or two text extracts. You must print these out before you begin work. See page v for guidance on how to do this.

You will practice important techniques such as:

ANNOTATION
Before completing your answers, mark up text extracts by:
- Underlining key quotations.
- Boxing off sub-sections of text that are the focus of a particular question, using the line references given.
- Annotating specific language and structure techniques used by the writer to consider their effect for Question 3.
- Annotating aspects of:
  - Setting
  - Incidents/Issues
  - Themes
  - Events

to evaluate the writer's success in relation to the question focus for Question 4.

Examiner tip
Do not use less than 45 minutes on the Writing question. Remember that it is worth 50% of this paper.

Examiner tip
Shorter questions may take you less time, which will leave some extra time for the longer questions 3 and 4.

Examiner tip
In the exam you must also annotate the questions; underline key words to keep your answer linked to the question focus.

CHECKING YOUR WORK
You must keep a final 5 minutes to check your written work. Make sure you have answered the question asked, selected relevant quotation(s) and written clear responses.

TIMING
Managing your time for each question will help you be successful.

PLANNING TECHNIQUES
For Writing responses.

Preparing for your exams

Paper 1 Question 1

Assessment objectives
- To find information (part of AO1)

Texts
This section uses the source text, *Varney the Vampire or the Feast of Blood* (1847).

What is the examiner looking for?
Question 1 checks if you can locate information in a text. To answer the question correctly, you need to:

- read the question carefully and follow the instruction to select one phrase
- find the shortest quotation that fully answers the question
- pinpoint the correct quotation rather than copying out long sections of the source.

Question format
Question 1 will always begin with the following words:

> From lines [….], identify a phrase which…

It might ask you to find information about a **person**, **thing**, **setting**, **action** or **event**.

For example:

> From lines 1–5, identify a phrase which shows that Pip feels anxious.   **(Total for Question 1 = 1 mark)**

Timing
Before completing Question 1 you should spend five minutes reading and understanding the text extract.

| Question 1 | 1 mark | 2 minutes |

You might find that this straightforward question takes less time. Make sure you check your answer and then bank any extra time for the longer answer questions.

Key steps

| Underline the key words in the question – the line references, the key search term 'phrase', and the focus you are looking for. | ▶ | Use your pen to box off the sub-extract defined by the question, using the line references at the side of the margin. | ▶ | Underline the shortest relevant phrase in the source text that fully answers the question. | ▶ | Copy out your short quotation. |

126

Paper 1 Question 1

Linked source text: *Varney the Vampire or the Feast of Blood* (1847)

Varney the Vampire or the Feast of Blood is an early gothic vampire story, first published as a weekly serial in cheap leaflets called 'Penny Dreadfuls'. Before considering the worked example and activities below, read the full extract, giving yourself the full five minutes to understand character, setting and action. Check the glossary for unfamiliar words and use the surrounding text to make an intelligent guess for any other words you don't know.

Candidate has identified key words in the question.

Worked example

From lines 3–10, identify a phrase which shows what was keeping the door fastened. **(1 mark)**

'Push it!' cried he who was using the bar, 'push the door at the same time.'

The younger man did so. For a few moments the massive door resisted. Then, suddenly, something gave way with a loud snap—it was a part of the lock,—and the door at once swung wide open. (5)

'It opens—it opens,' cried the young man.

'Another moment,' said the stranger, as he still plied the crowbar—'another moment, and we shall have free ingress to the chamber. Be patient.' (10)

This stranger's name was Marchdale; and even as he spoke, he succeeded in throwing the massive door wide open, and clearing the passage to the chamber.

Candidate has 'boxed off' the correct sub-extract indicated in the question.

Candidate has underlined the relevant phrase before writing out their answer.

Examiner tip

The exam paper will include line references every 5 lines of a printed source text. You must know how to work out the line numbers for each line in between so you can follow the instructions in the question.

Student answer: it was a part of the lock

The exact answer has been given. ✓

Building your skills

Activity 1

Look at the questions below which have been annotated by a student. Which candidate has annotated the questions most accurately, keeping to the guidance from page 125, to give them the best chance of getting full marks? Give reasons for your answer.

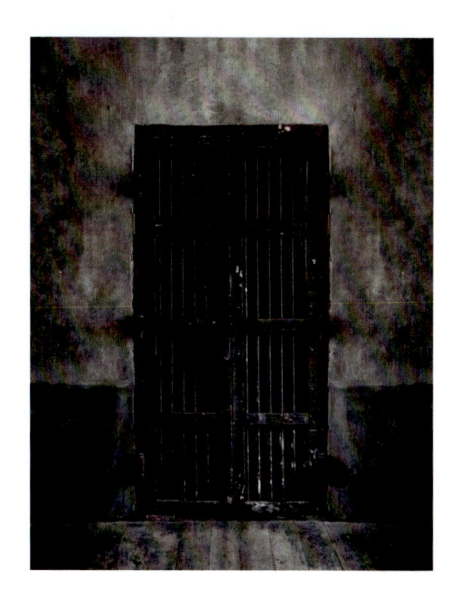

127

Preparing for your exams

Candidate A	From lines 1–5, identify a phrase which shows that Pip feels anxious.	From lines 11–16, identify a phrase which describes what happens to the sky when the weather changes.	From lines 1–5, identify the phrase which explains why the children have nothing to eat.
Candidate B	From lines 1–5, identify a phrase which shows that Pip feels anxious.	From lines 11–16, identify a phrase which describes what happens to the sky when the weather changes.	From lines 1–5, identify the phrase which explains why the children have nothing to eat.
Candidate C	From lines 1–5, identify a phrase which shows that Pip feels anxious.	From lines 11–16, identify a phrase which describes what happens to the sky when the weather changes.	From lines 1–5, identify the phrase which explains why the children have nothing to eat.

Activity 2

Now apply the skills you have learned to answer these example exam-style questions on the next section of *Varney the Vampire or the Feast of Blood*. Refer to the Key steps on page 126 to help you.

> **Examiner tip**
>
> Remember to check that your answer is from within the line references stated in the question.

1 From lines 14–20, identify a phrase which explains why Henry's candle did not provide enough light.

1 From lines 22–25, identify the phrase which suggests that the intruder in the room moved quickly.

1 From lines 30–34, identify a phrase which describes the intruder as frightening.

Activity 3

1. Read the final section of the extract and consider the student answers to the exam-style question below. Mark each student answer as correct or incorrect. Write a phrase explaining your marking, based on the skills you have learned for Question 1.

   > 1 From lines 38–42, select a phrase which explains why Mr Marchdale was able to act more quickly than his companion.
   > **(1 mark)**

   Candidate A   a man of mature years

   Candidate B   was much more likely to recover sooner than his younger companions

   Candidate C   he had seen much of life

2. Create your own sample Question 1 based on a section of the extract. Give it to a partner to answer.

Paper 1 Question 2

Assessment objectives
- To identify and interpret explicit and implicit information (part of AO1)

Texts
This section uses the source text *Good Lady Ducayne* by Mary Elizabeth Braddon (1896).

What is the examiner looking for?
Question 2 asks you to find obvious (explicit) information as well as what is being suggested (implicit information). It also tests your ability to read the question and follow instructions carefully by locating a sub-section of the text. You must copy out two quotations or use your own words.

Question format
Question 2 will always begin with the following words:

From lines […], give **two** ways…

Read the example question below.

2   From lines 8–14, give **two** ways in which the writer shows that Eric is not a good sportsman. You may use your own words or quotations from the text.

   1   ....
   2   ....

(Total for Question 2 = 2 marks)

Timing

| Question 2 | 2 marks | 4 minutes | (2 minutes per mark) |

This straightforward question may take less time. Check you have taken your answer from the correct sub-extract. Then save any extra time for the longer answer questions.

Key steps

Underline the key words in the question – the line references, the key search term and the focus you are looking for.

▶ Mark the sub-extract on the source text, using the line references at the side of the margin.

▶ Underline the key words in the source text.

▶ Copy out your two short quotations directly from the source, if you can. If not, adjust them slightly using some of your own words.

Linked source text: *Good Lady Ducayne* by Mary Elizabeth Braddon (1896)

Activity 1

Before tackling any reading questions in Paper 1 you should spend 5 minutes reading and understanding the extract. Practise these skills using a printout of the full extract from *Good Lady Ducayne*.

1. Read the full extract giving yourself five minutes to understand character, setting and action.

2. With a partner, check that you share a common understanding of the story. Give yourself five minutes to discuss the story, using the prompts below and evidence from the text.

   - Where is this story set?
   - What has brought these two women together?
   - What do you know about Bella's social background?
   - What impression do you get of the female interviewer and why?
   - What impression do you get of Bella and why?

Worked example

> [...] five solid shillings had been handed to a smartly-dressed lady in an office in Harbeck Street, W., in the hope that this very Superior Person would find a situation and a salary for Miss Rolleston. The Superior Person glanced at the two half-crowns as they lay on the table where Bella's hand had placed them, to make sure they were neither of them forms, before she wrote a description of Bella's qualifications and requirements in a formidable-looking ledger.   (5)

2 From lines 5–8, give two ways in which the writer shows that the Superior Person is interested in financial profit.

Key words of the question annotated correctly. ✓

1 "glanced at the two half-crowns"

Relevant quotation lifted from the text. ✓

2 she checked the money was real before she wrote down Bella's details

Paraphrased relevant example. ✓

Building your skills

Activity 2

The exam paper allows direct quotations or paraphrasing. Paraphrasing means putting the information from the text into your own words. If you do this, be careful not to change the original meaning.

1. Read the paraphrased student answers below. Select the two most accurate statements.

> 2 From lines 16–19, give **two** ways in which the writer shows that Bella is not impressive in her interview. You may use your own words or quotations from the text.

   i) She says she used to play the piano.
   ii) She admits she has forgotten how to play the piano.
   iii) She adds she has not spent any time studying.
   iv) She says she has not spent very much time studying.

2. Now use quotations instead of paraphrasing. Copy out the two shortest quotations from the passage that fully answer the question.

> **Examiner tip**
> Keep quotations precise. You do not need to embed them in full sentences. Copying out large chunks of text will not be rewarded in the exam.

Activity 3

1. Now apply the skills you have learned to answer this exam-style question on the next section of *Good Lady Ducayne*. Refer to the Key steps on page 129 to help you.

> 2 From lines 33–38 give **two** ways the writer suggests the interviewer seems rather strange. You may use your own words or quotations from the text. **(2 marks)**

2. Write your own exam Question 2 based on the extract. Give your question to a partner to answer.

Preparing for your exams

Paper 1 Question 3

Assessment objectives

- Explain, comment on and analyse how writers use language and structure to achieve effects and influence readers, using relevant subject terminology to support their views (AO2)

Texts

This section uses the source text *The Kiss* by Kate Chopin (1895).

What is the examiner looking for?

Question 3 is a longer answer question. You must identify the writer's choices of language and structure and explain their effects. The question asks you to focus on a sub-section of the text. Your points must:

- link to the focus of the question
- use textual references
- analyse their effect on the reader
- focus on **both** language and structure.

Question format

Question 3 will always begin with the following words:

In lines […], how does the writer use language and structure to […]

Read the example questions below.

> **3** In lines 26–37 how does the writer use language and structure to show the narrator's feelings about his family? Support your views with reference to the text.
>
> (Total for Question 3 = 6 marks)

> **3** From lines 20–28 how does the writer use language and structure to show the change in the mood of the partygoers? Support your views with reference to the text.
>
> (Total for Question 3 = 6 marks)

Timing

| Question 3 | 6 marks | 12 minutes | (2 minutes per mark) |

Paper 1 Question 3

Key steps

Mark the sub-extract on the source text using the line references at the side of the margin. ▶ Underline the key words in the question (the line references and the focus). ▶ Annotate the sub-extract. Mark language and structural features. Think about their effect in relation to the question focus. ▶ Write your answer, using concise Point, Evidence, Explanation for 3–4 points. Make sure you have points on both language and structure.

Linked source text: *The Kiss* by Kate Chopin (1895)

Worked example

Activity 1

1. Read the extract from *The Kiss* by Kate Chopin independently. Then share your thoughts with a partner and agree your understanding of why the characters behave as they do in the story.

   In the exam you must include aspects of **both language *and* structure**. The author uses a range of these features to convey the characters' feelings about each other. In the exam, annotating the extract will help you to identify how the author has used features of language and structure.

2. The first half of the extract has been annotated for you. Continue the annotations using a printout of the story. How many features can you identify in the final section?

   - Use the checklist below to support you.
   - Pay attention to sentence types and lengths in the final section.

Language and structure – a checklist

Language	Structure
• Interesting choices of vocabulary • Figurative language (simile, metaphor) • Imagery • Personification • Word classes: nouns, verbs, adjectives, adverbs • Repetition of words (in close proximity) • Dialogue and its style: informal and formal language, dialect	• Beginning–middle–end • Shifts in time/place/character/mood/atmosphere/attitudes • Shifts at the beginning/middle/end of the section • Repetition of words, phrases, ideas across the extract • Punctuation, for example, question marks, ellipses, exclamations, pauses, time connectives • The balance of description versus dialogue • Sentence types (minor, simple, compound, complex) • Sentence lengths (short, long) • Foreshadowing/predicting • 'Zooming in' – moving from a wider view to focus on precise details • 'Zooming out' – moving from a narrow view to the bigger picture

133

Preparing for your exams

It was still quite light out of doors, but inside with the curtains drawn and the smouldering fire sending out a dim, uncertain glow, the room was full of deep shadows.

Brantain sat in one of these shadows; it had overtaken him and he did not mind. The obscurity lent him courage to keep his (5) eyes fastened as ardently* as he liked upon the girl who sat in the firelight.

She was very handsome, with a certain fine, rich coloring that belongs to the healthy brune* type. She was quite composed, as she idly stroked the satiny coat of the cat that lay curled in (10) her lap, and she occasionally sent a slow glance into the shadow where her companion sat. They were talking low, of indifferent things which plainly were not the things that occupied their thoughts. She knew that he loved her—a frank, blustering fellow without guile* enough to conceal his feelings, and no desire to (15) do so. For two weeks past he had sought her society* eagerly and persistently. She was confidently waiting for him to declare himself* and she meant to accept him. The rather insignificant and unattractive Brantain was enormously rich; and she liked and required the entourage which wealth could give her. (20)

Annotations:
- **figurative language** – his obsession with her appearance
- **common noun** rather than her name – emphasises the importance of her gender for this relationship/marriage
- **shift of focus** – contrasts their very different thoughts
- **descriptive language/range of adjectives** – her attractiveness
- **time connective** – she's less interested in looking at him
- **sibilance** – suggests flirting
- **shift** – at this point

Glossary

Ardently: With passion

Brune: Brunette (brown)

Guile: Cunning, slyness

Declare himself: Propose marriage to her

Society: company, friendship

Activity 2

Question 3 also tests your ability to explain the *effect* of language and structure in relation to the question focus. Notice the underlined text in the student answer below where the student mentions the **effect** of the devices.

1. Read lines 21–36 of *The Kiss* together with the first half of the student answer below.

> **3** From lines 21–36 how does the writer use language and structure to show Brantain's change in mood?

The writer begins the paragraph with the same intimate mood between Brantain and the girl. The use of the noun phrase 'one of the pauses' <u>shows that the romantic atmosphere continues</u>. However, there is a turning point early on in this paragraph as 'the door opened'; A second man entering the room <u>breaks the romantic mood and provides a contrast</u>. The writer's use of a long complex sentence in lines 24-27 after a simple sentence 'The girl turned her face towards him' <u>shows a change in energy</u>. The long sentence focuses on his shocking action of kissing the girl. <u>The effect of this is to change Brantain's mood from romance to tension.</u>

The student has focused on structural features in this answer – there is not enough attention to language.

2. Complete the following points about language. Identify the effect of each feature in relation to the question focus, 'Brantain's change in mood'.

The writer uses the adverb 'slowly'. The effect of this is to…

The repetition of the first person 'I' in lines 31–32 conveys the idea that Brantain…

The description of Brantain as 'clutching' is also important…

> **Examiner tip**
>
> You do not have to separate language features and structural features in your answer. However you do need to know that you have covered both aspects.

Activity 3

1. Read through the criteria of a successful Question 3 answer below.

   - Points about structure
   - Points about language
   - 3–4 points in relation to the question
   - Relevant quotations or line references
   - Short PEA points
   - Explanation of the effect of features in relation to the question
   - Identification of specific points of information in relation to the question focus
   - Using literary terms

2. Now read the sub-extract, question and student answer below.

   > 3 In lines 37–56, how does the writer use language and structure to show the girl's character? Support your views with reference to the text. **(6 marks)**

   In this extract the girl seems anxious and desperate but really this is all an act that allows her to get what she wants. The writer uses polite language in her speech to show how she tries to seem humble and pleading to Brantain when really she is trying to make him interested in her again. The writer's descriptive language for Brantain mentions his 'guileless face'. The effect of this is to show how she has the power and he is convinced by her words even though he saw another man kiss her. The shift in the passage occurs as her mood matches Brantain's; they both move from seeming unhappy.

Preparing for your exams

3. Using the criteria in task 1 above, identify the changes that need to be made to the student answer to achieve full marks. Now rewrite the answer to achieve full marks.

Activity 4

Apply the skills you have learned to answer the exam question below. Refer to the formula in the tip box to help you write a high quality answer.

> **3** From lines 66–75, how does the writer use language and structure to show Miss Nathalie as less powerful than she originally seemed? **(6 marks)**

Examiner tip

One method of ensuring a balanced answer, addressing both language and structure, is to use the formula below to identify features and their effect:

- one comment on vocabulary
- one comment on sentences
- identify any structural shift or change of focus
- add one or two more relevant points from the language and structure diagrams on page 133.

Paper 1 Question 4

Assessment objectives
- To evaluate texts critically and support this with appropriate textual references (AO4)

Texts
This section uses two source texts: *Lady Audley's Secret* by Mary Elizabeth Braddon (1896) and *The Yellow Sign* by Robert W. Chambers (1895).

What is the examiner looking for?
Question 4 is a longer answer that focuses on evaluating the *whole* extract. Evaluating means looking at the 'bigger picture'. Question 4 asks you to judge the success of the text, concentrating on an aspect the writer is trying to achieve. Your judgement should be supported by evidence. It does not require you to analyse evidence in extended detail.

Examiner tip
The focus of evaluation is upon how *well* something has been achieved, not merely upon how it has been achieved.

Examiner tip
Remember, you are evaluating the writing of established nineteenth-century authors. You are not aiming to criticise the writer but to appreciate their skill.

Question format
Question 4 will always begin with the following words:

> In this extract, there is an attempt to […]. Evaluate how successfully this is achieved. Support your views with detailed reference to the text.

The focus of the question will vary. Examples might include questions about ideas, character or mood. Read the example question below.

4 In this extract, there is an attempt to show Peter's understanding of the way that family life works. Evaluate how successfully this is achieved. Support your views with detailed reference to the text.

(Total for Question 4 = 15 marks)

Timing

| Question 4 | 15 marks | 30 minutes | (2 minutes per mark) |

Remember, this is a longer answer worth many marks. Make sure you leave enough time to complete your answer. You are given two sides of the answer booklet for your writing. You can ask for more paper, but two sides should be enough for a quality full-mark answer.

Preparing for your exams

Key steps

| Underline the key words in the question – particularly the key focus of your evaluation. | ▶ | Move **chronologically** through the source text, . Mark up where the author focuses on **S**etting, **I**deas, **T**hemes and **E**vents. | ▶ | Decide on a short summary statement in response to the key focus of your evaluation. | ▶ | Write your answer, beginning with a short summary statement and moving chronologically through the text to evaluate SITE using examples. | ▶ | Read your answer again and check you have used positive evaluative language. |

📄 Linked source text: *Lady Audley's Secret* by Mary Elizabeth Braddon (1896)

Activity 1

1. Before you begin, remind yourself of the aspects of evaluating a text. You learned about using SITE or TIES, as a method of checking how the writer attempts to show something, in Unit 6, page 69. Copy the table below, and explain what you are looking for when evaluating. The first row has been completed for you.

SITE aspect	What I am looking for
Setting	Places and what they are like. Any changes of place. E.g. Outside or inside. Weather. Temperature. What they look like. Nature. Night or day.
Ideas and Incidents	
Themes	
Events	

2. Read the full extract of *Lady Audley's Secret*. Once you have done this, agree your understanding of the text with a partner.
   - What is the relationship between the two women?
   - What crime has been committed?
   - Who may have done this?

Worked example

Consider the question below in relation to *Lady Audley's Secret*.

Responding to Question 4 requires you to do two key things.

- Annotate the text clearly to identify aspects of SITE.
- Write this up as a longer answer.

> **Examiner tip**
>
> You do not need to write about every paragraph of the text if you have not found something relevant to the question focus in a particular section.

> **4** In this extract, there is an attempt to show how criminals are sometimes the most unexpected people. Evaluate how successfully this is achieved. Support your views with detailed reference to the text.
>
> (Total for Question 4 = 15 marks)

138

Paper 1 Question 4

Read through the student annotations and response below. Notice how the annotations on the source text reflect the content of the answer.

She took the girl's arm, and half led, half dragged her from the house. The convulsive pressure of her slight hand held her firmly as an iron vice could have held her. The fierce March wind banged to the door of the house, and left the two women standing outside it. The long, black road lay bleak and desolate before them, dimly visible between straight lines of leafless hedges.	(5)	SITE (circled) Incident – dragging her Incident/idea – violent Setting – threatening SITE (circled)
A walk of three miles' length upon a lonely country road, between the hours of two and four on a cold winter's morning, is scarcely a pleasant task for a delicate woman – a woman whose inclinations lean toward ease and luxury. But my lady hurried along the hard, dry highway, dragging her companion with her as if she had been impelled by some horrible demoniac force which knew no abatement. With the black night above them – with the fierce wind howling around them, sweeping across a broad expanse of hidden country, blowing as if it had arisen simultaneously from every point of the compass, and making those wanderers the focus of its ferocity – the two women walked through the darkness down the hill upon which Mount Stanning stood, along a mile and a half of flat road, and then up another hill, on the western side of which Audley Court lay in that sheltered valley, which seemed to shut in the old house from all the clamour and hubbub of the everyday world.	(10) (15) (20)	setting emphasised – dangerous incident/ideas – action of dragging – aggressive theme of danger setting – privileged
My lady stopped upon the summit of this hill to draw breath and to clasp her hands upon her heart, in the vain hope that she might still its cruel beating. They were now within three-quarters of a mile of the Court, and they had been walking for nearly an hour since they had left the Castle Inn. Lady Audley stopped to rest, with her face still turned toward the place of her destination. Phoebe Marks, stopping also, and very glad of a moment's pause in that hurried journey, looked back into the far darkness beneath which lay that dreary shelter that had given her so much uneasiness. And she did so, she uttered a shrill cry of horror, and clutched wildly at her companion's cloak.	(25) (30)	theme is isolation – women alone in the middle of the two places theme of danger and safety incident/ideas link to incident

139

Preparing for your exams

Overall in this extract the writer encourages the reader to think about crime and criminals since at the beginning it seems the women could be victims of crime but by the end the writer surprisingly suggests the upper class woman is the (criminal.) In the (first paragraph) the (setting) works well to make the reader feel that the women are vulnerable. The fact that they are walking in the dark and alone is successful in creating tension about possible crime – 'the long, black road lay bleak and desolate'. The theme of danger begins with the setting but is also developed by the incident of the older woman dragging her servant with the words ('iron vice') suggesting force. The way she behaves is a bit surprising so this works (well) in making the reader feel uneasy about this upper class woman. The second paragraph continues this (idea,) successfully presenting the women as potential victims. It reminds us how Lady Audley comes from a world that is protected from crime and danger. The setting of Audley Court in a 'sheltered valley' suggests that she is separate from others, probably because of her status. The setting of the road definitely seems dangerous with words associated with darkness and demons ('black...horrible demoniac force'). The themes of danger and evil are continued by the author, emphasising the women being alone and in the dark, calling Lady Audley 'delicate' and reminding us of her 'ease and luxury'.

✓ short opening that establishes the focus of the question and your reading of it in summary across the extract
✓ moves chronologically through the passage
✓ setting
✓ evidence
✓ evidence
✓ positive evaluative language
✓ idea

Activity 2

1. Look at the annotations on the final paragraph of the extract on page 139. Write the next paragraph of this student's evaluation. Remember to:

    - keep to the question focus of 'criminals being the most unexpected people'
    - use evaluative language to make a positive judgement
    - use short embedded textual references
    - consider all aspects of SITE, but only write about the most significant aspects.

   Examiner tip
   A text with lots of dialogue will not necessarily be divided into neat paragraphs. You can still move through the text chronologically and divide it up logically to evaluate.

2. Complete the response to the question on *Lady Audley's Secret* by annotating a copy of the next section of text and then writing the final section of the answer.

Paper 1 Question 4

Activity 3

Evaluation requires you to make a judgement. Since these are published fiction texts, the assumption is that the writing is high quality. So make a judgement, but make it positive!

Read over the student answer above plus your own response and find all the examples of evaluative language. Make your own word bank like the one below.

Evaluative language bank
works well

> **Examiner tip**
>
> Some students prefer to show evidence of evaluation by linking their judgements to a first person perspective using 'I'. For example:
>
> I think this is a particularly skilful way of suggesting that Lady Audley has negative qualities.

> **Examiner tip**
>
> As you go through your answer, make sure there are times when you say *how well* something has been done.

Activity 4

The evaluation question focuses on the big picture. Ideally you should also add a very brief section that shows your understanding of how language and structure contribute to the writer's success. Remember that you are focusing on overall impact rather than analysing the details of how devices work.

1. Read the following extract from the end of the student answer on *Lady Audley's Secret,* which focuses on how the text's **structure** helps to convey the idea that criminals can be the most unexpected people:

   > As a whole, the structure of the passage cleverly moves from large to small, from the huge setting of the night landscape and then focusing in on Lady Audley. It is rather like a detective, looking at the whole picture, and then finally finding the criminal, definitely an unexpected one, which is Lady Audley.

2. Now add a final section focusing on how the text's **language** helps to convey the idea that criminals can be the most unexpected people. Use the sentence starter below to help you.

   > Overall the language of this passage artfully moves from dark to light...

141

Preparing for your exams

Activity 5

Before you write a complete answer to a Question 4, remind yourself of the key features you have learned.

Read the statements below about how to answer Question 4. Decide if they are true or false.

	Statement
1	I should remember to use words that gently praise the skill of what the writer has done.
2	I should identify the setting, incidents, themes and events in every paragraph.
3	I should identify at least one aspect of each paragraph to evaluate, such as setting, incidents, themes or events.
4	I should write a detailed introduction and conclusion.
5	I should begin with a general overall statement that establishes what the writer is doing in relation to the question focus.
6	I should include detailed language analysis for each point I make.
7	I must remember that evaluate means looking at the bigger picture.
8	I should track logically through each section of the text.
9	I should keep only to the lines specified in the question rather than reading the whole text.
10	I should include some evidence from the text.

Linked source text: *The Yellow Sign* by Robert W. Chambers (1895)

Activity 6

Now apply all these skills to your own evaluation of another unseen extract. Remember to:

- Read and understand the passage in 5 minutes.
- Annotate the sections using SITE, keeping the question focus in mind.
- Write up your answer, beginning with an opening summary statement and moving chronologically through the text to evaluate SITE using examples.
- Refer back to the question focus regularly.
- Use evaluative language.
- End with a brief overall comment about language and structure.

Read the extract from *The Yellow Sign* by Robert W. Chambers and answer the exam-style question below.

> 4   In this extract, there is an attempt to build a sense of threat. Evaluate how successfully this is achieved. Support your views with detailed reference to the text.
>
> (Total for Question 4 = 15 marks)

Paper 1 Questions 5 & 6

Assessment objectives

- Communicate clearly, effectively and imaginatively, selecting and adapting tone, style and register for different forms, purposes and audiences. Organise information and ideas, using structural and grammatical features to support coherence and cohesion of texts. (AO5)
- Use a range of vocabulary and sentence structures for clarity, purpose and effect, with accurate spelling and punctuation. (AO6)

Questions 5 and 6 assess your ability to write **imaginatively** and **creatively.**

You only need to answer one question: either Question 5 or Question 6. One question will always include some pictures which you can use for inspiration.

The examiner will be looking for:

- organised writing which reads well and is engaging
- evidence that you have thought about the voice and tone of your piece
- accurate spelling, punctuation and grammar
- correct use of a wide range of words and sentence structures.

Question format

Question 5 will always begin with the following words:

> Look at the images provided. Write about a time when […]

Question 6 will always begin with the following words:

> Write about a time when […]

Both questions might mention you or someone you know or just ask something about you. You might be asked to focus on an event, a feeling, a location or an experience.

In Question 5, you can use the images provided to help you but you don't have to.

Both questions will also have an asterisk (*) next to them and a line underneath reminding you about your spelling and grammar.

Preparing for your exams

Read the example questions below.

EITHER

*5 Look at the images provided. Write about your hopes for the future. Your response could be real or imagined. You may wish to base your response on one of the images.

....

....

(Total for Question 5 = 40 marks)

*Your response will be marked for the accurate and appropriate use of vocabulary, spelling, punctuation and grammar.

OR

*6 Write about a time when something surprising happened to you or someone you know. Your response could be real or imagined.

....

....

(Total for Question 6 = 40 marks)

*Your response will be marked for the accurate and appropriate use of vocabulary, spelling, punctuation and grammar.

Timing

Before completing Question 5 or 6, you should spend 5–10 minutes writing a plan. You will then have 30–35 minutes to write your response and 5 minutes to check your work at the end.

You have 45 minutes in total. Make sure you have left enough time to complete this question and aim to finish it in 40 minutes. Use the extra time to check your answer.

Paper 1 Questions 5 & 6

Key steps

Read both questions carefully and look at the images. Think about how you want to use the images in your answer. ▶ Decide which form (narrative, description or monologue) you are going to use. ▶ Choose a question.

Check your response and make any changes that are necessary. Be careful and do not make too many unnecessary changes. ◀ Write your response using your plan. Use it as a guide to help shape each paragraph and maintain the form of the piece. ◀ Spend 5–10 minutes planning your work. Make sure you are clear about how you are going to start and finish your piece of work.

Voice and form in Questions 5 and 6

There are three main forms you can choose to write in for Questions 5 and 6 and you will need to decide which to use before you begin to plan and write. This will help you to decide which question to choose.

> **Examiner tip**
>
> Ideas about how to write a description using a picture as inspiration can be found in Unit 8.1 In the frame: Using pictures to write creatively.

Form 1: Narrative

A narrative is a series of events or a specific event – a story. It can be fictional or true. It can be based on your own experiences or those of somebody else.

Form 2: Monologue

A monologue is written in the first person and reflects the inner thoughts and feelings of a person.

Form 3: Description

A description paints a picture of a single moment and can focus on a location, scene or person. This is when you might want to use one of the pictures provided in the exam to help shape your description.

Activity 1

1. Look at the three following examples, and decide if they are narrative, monologue or description. Identify the phrases or words in the examples and explain why you think they are that form.

> **Example**
>
> **Candidate A:**
>
> I often sit at my window and watch the world go by. It is amazing how you can set your watch by other people. I know it is 8:30 when I see the lady next door leave her house and I hear her dog barking. Once she has gone, the students who live opposite me leave their house to get to their lectures on time. As I watch everyone leave the house for the day, I think to myself 'Why can't that be me? Why am I stuck here all day?'

> **Candidate B:**
> The castle loomed majestically on the horizon. Its turrets were a deep black colour that glistened in the moonlight. The windows were hardly visible in the darkness apart from a small, bright light that shone like a lone star from the upstairs window.

> **Candidate C:**
> The first bad decision we made was when we decided to climb the hill to the nearest house as the car had run out of petrol. As we struggled up the increasingly steep path, we realised that it was getting colder and colder with every step. By the time we were at the half way point, we spied a church and decided to shelter in there for a few moments. This was the second bad decision.

2. Look again at the two example exam questions on page 144. Spend five minutes making some notes about how you would answer one of the questions in the form of a narrative, monologue or description.

Planning your work

It is really important that you write a plan **before** you start writing. You don't need to spend too long on this, but it does need to be detailed enough to help you with your writing. Look back at Unit 7.6 for extra help with this. A good plan will help your writing have a very definite beginning, middle and end.

> **Examiner tip**
> A lack of planning and thinking ahead causes many students to lose marks. A good plan will ensure your writing reaches a clear end point.

Activity 2

The two students below have devised some shapes to fill in their plan in response to the following question:

> Write about a time when you or someone you know overcame a fear. **(40 marks)**

Which of these planning formats is likely to be more successful and why? What improvements would you make to each plan?

Student 1

When I was brave…

1….	2…	3…
4…	5…	6…

Student 2

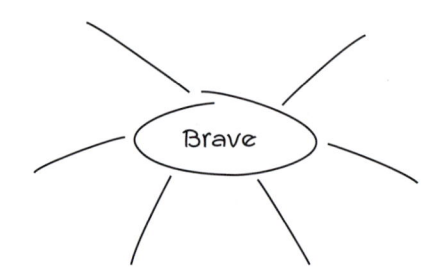

Brave (mind map)

Many students do not plan well. You need to label or number your plan to structure your writing in paragraphs. The example on the next page demonstrates the essential features of a plan.

> Write about a time when you or someone you know overcame a fear. **(40 marks)**

Paper 1 Questions 5 & 6

Plan	Annotations
Paragraph 1. Opening – set the scene. Nervous about making a speech at school. Describe the senses – 'feel like a storm is raging in my head.'	Establish setting and focus.
P2. Action – walk into the room. Short sentences for fear. Overcome my fear by thinking about my goal – raising money for charity.	Note some key devices. Purpose further explained. Clear purpose explained.
P3. Action – get to the podium. Forget words. Describe lights and the blur of the crowd. Time indicators to increase tension. 10 seconds passed, then 20, then 30…	
P4. Climax – See Emma in the crowd and remember why I am doing this. For charity to raise money for a good cause. Summon up courage and speak passionately about the cause.	Clear climax and turning point.
P5. End – finish on a high point. Speech was a success. Audience clapped. Describe the scene and feelings. Use senses from first paragraph but put a positive spin. Thoughts are calm – 'like waves lapping on the shore.'	Clearly defined end point links back to opening.

> **Examiner tip**
> Avoid using a brainstorm or spider diagram to plan your writing unless you number each point to reflect the order of your paragraphs.

Activity 3

Now write your own five-paragraph plan for the following exam question.

Write about a time when you or someone you know won something. **(40 marks)**

Openings

Most good stories have a distinctive opening and there are a number of ways in which you can ensure that your imaginative writing is memorable for all the right reasons. It is also important to establish the tone of your writing as soon as you start, as this will help with your overall mark for AO5.

> **Examiner tip**
> Don't be afraid to change the order of the boxes to help you. You might want to start or finish with a very dramatic moment or add more paragraphs.

In the extracts you will have read to prepare for the exam, you will have noticed that there are many different and engaging ways to start a piece of writing. They all aim to engage the reader from the start and this is something that you must try to do for the examiner. Here are some ideas.

Opening 1: Dialogue

Direct speech can open a narrative by establishing character and/or action. For example, *"This is a disaster!" Michelle wailed.*

Preparing for your exams

Opening 2: Action

Opening a story in the middle of the action can immediately engage your reader. For example, *My body began to sink as the waves grew stronger.*

Opening 3: Description

This would be expected with a descriptive piece. Using description to establish setting can also work well with narrative or monologue. For example, *The beach was like a thin fingernail of grey stones. Desolate. Dead.*

Opening 4: Intrigue

Open your piece of writing in an unusual way that creates questions in the reader's mind. Try to resolve these questions by the end of the second or third paragraphs. For example, *I always knew he was going to disappear.*

Activity 4

1. Match the different types of opening listed above to the different examples below. Identify phrases or words from the examples to explain why you think they are that type of opening.

Example
Candidate A: The sunrise was the most beautiful thing I had ever seen. The darkness slowly subsided and was taken over by a strong, powerful and warming light. The birds started to sing; the stream sparkled and the flowers began to bloom.
Candidate B: 'So, my name is Chloe and I will be looking after you today,' she said in a comforting tone as she bent over the patient. 'How are you feeling?' Daniel opened his eyes and instantly felt the pain from his head wound. 'I feel terrible' he groaned.
Candidate C: I will never forget the day when they arrived at our house. They were wearing black clothes and just walked in without invitation. No one stopped them. No one saw them arrive. It was as if they just floated in from another planet.
Candidate D: Bang! The gun went off and I sped off as if my life depended on it. I had to get to that door before it closed and seek refuge from the barrage of gunfire going off around me.

2. Select one of the openings and think about how you would develop the story. Make a plan and then compare your ideas with a partner. Think of ways to improve each other's plans.

Remind yourself of the task.

> Write about a time when you or someone you know won something. **(40 marks)**

3. Complete the middle of the story you have chosen.

Endings

Just as with openings, good stories have to have a good ending. They can show how all of the issues or actions are resolved, or they can surprise the reader with an unexpected ending. Some stories end on a cliffhanger, which leaves the reader in suspense. Most importantly, endings allow the reader to bring together all of the ideas which have been mentioned in the imaginative piece and to feel there is a conclusion to them – whether it is 'satisfying' or not.

There are many different ways to end an imaginative piece of writing.

> **Examiner tip**
>
> If you have planned properly, you should have time to write a successful ending to your piece.
>
> It is very important that your imaginative writing has an ending which makes sense to the reader and allows the examiner to award the AO5 mark.

Ending 1: A cliffhanger

A cliffhanger allows you to end at a climactic point. It has to be planned for carefully so that the examiner is convinced that the ending is planned, and not a result of poor timekeeping in the exam.

Ending 2: A satisfying ending

This offers a clear resolution. You might want to echo a word, phrase or image from your opening to provide a neat conclusion.

Ending 3: A surprise ending

A surprise ending should of course surprise your reader, but you need to plan this very carefully so that it makes sense and is believable.

Preparing for your exams

Activity 5

1. Look again at the openings on page 147–148 and think about the potential endings these stories might have, using the suggestions above. Make a table like the one below to list your ideas. The first one has been completed for you.

Example opening	Example ending	
Candidate A: The sunrise was the most beautiful thing I had ever seen. The darkness slowly subsided and was taken over by a strong, powerful and warming light. The birds started to sing; the stream sparkled and the flowers began to bloom.	The day was over. The light was slowly disappearing and the beautiful, clear sky was being taken over by the gloom. The birds were silenced for the day; the stream became eerily dark in the moonlight and the blooms closed to become green buds.	The end of the day emphasises it is the end of the piece. Use of opposites (in the disappearing light and silence of birds) mirrors the style of opening.
Candidate B: 'So, my name is Chloe and I will be looking after you today,' she said in a comforting tone as she bent over the patient. 'How are you feeling?' Daniel opened his eyes and instantly felt the pain from his head wound. 'I feel terrible' he groaned.		
Candidate C: I will never forget the day when they arrived at our house. They were wearing black clothes and just walked in without invitation. No one stopped them. No one saw them arrive. It was as if they just floated in from another planet.		
Candidate D: Bang! The gun went off and I sped off as if my life depended on it. I had to get to that door before it closed and seek refuge from the barrage of gunfire going off around me.		

2. Go back to the plan you wrote in Activity 3 on page 147. Complete this plan making sure you include a strong opening and ending.

3. Now write your story, following your plan carefully.

Checking your work

Once you have written your piece of writing, it is essential that you check it for spelling, punctuation and grammar. You must make sure there are no errors in these areas. You might want to write your whole piece of writing and check everything at the end, or do it as you write and check each paragraph as you go. There is no right or wrong way to do this, as long as you do leave time to check your work.

> **Examiner tip**
>
> Once you have finished your writing, it is essential that you check it for written accuracy. Students who fail to do this will lose marks for AO6.

Activity 6

This student needs to check her work for spelling, punctuation and grammar. Read through what she has written and note down where mistakes have been made. Rewrite and try to improve the paragraph by correcting the mistakes.

> **Candidate C:**
>
> The girls new she had to escape but which way should she turn. Every root was blocked and their seemed to be now way out. She tried the door again twisting the handle first one way then the other. No luck. So she tried to use the lampshade to break the window it cracked a bit but she needed to hit it a bit harder again and again for it to make any difference. Did she have the strength. She had to get out now.

Preparing for your exams: Paper 2

Exam guidance

Exam technique: Paper 2 Fiction and Imaginative Writing

What is it worth?

Paper 2 is worth **60%** of your English Language GCSE.

There are two sections which are each worth 50% of the total marks for this paper:

Paper 2 Section A: Reading = 50%   Paper 2 Section B: Writing = 50%

What does it test?

Section A questions test all four Reading Assessment Objectives:

AO1	• Identify and interpret explicit and implicit information and ideas • Select and synthesise evidence from different texts
AO2	Explain, comment on and analyse how writers use language and structure to achieve effects and influence readers, using relevant subject terminology to support their views
AO3	Compare writers' ideas and perspectives, as well as how these are conveyed, across two or more texts
AO4	Evaluate texts critically and support this with appropriate textual references

Section B questions address both Writing Assessment Objectives:

AO5	• Communicate clearly, effectively and imaginatively, selecting and adapting tone, style and register for different forms, purposes and audiences. • Organise information and ideas, using structural and grammatical features to support coherence and cohesion of texts
AO6	Use a range of vocabulary and sentence structures for clarity, purpose and effect, with accurate spelling and punctuation

What does the paper contain?

Section A: Reading presents unseen non-fiction extracts, **one 20th- and one 21st-century text** totalling around 1000 words. It contains 8 questions.

Text 1	Questions 1 and 2 (2 marks each)	Ask you to identify explicit information (AO1)
	Question 3 (15 marks)	Asks you to focus on language and structure (AO2)
Text 2	Questions 4 and 5 (1 mark each)	Ask you to identify explicit information (AO1)
	Question 6 (15 marks)	Asks you to evaluate Text 2 in relation to a given focus (AO4)
Both texts	Questions 7a (6 marks) and 7b (14 marks)	Ask you to synthesis and then compare information across both texts (AO3)

152

Exam technique: Paper 2 Fiction and Imaginative Writing

Section B: Transactional Writing asks you to choose one task from a choice of two.

You will be asked to write a text in a particular form, such as a magazine or newspaper article, letter, report, text book extract, review or obituary. Writing tasks are linked by a theme to the reading extracts. It is possible for the same form (for example, a letter or an article) to be set by both tasks in the same paper but with a different focus and/or audience. Writing must show clear organisation and structure with an opening, development of points and a conclusion.

What is the timing?

Paper 2 = two hours and 5 minutes in total.

- 80 minutes on the Reading Section
- 45 minutes on the Writing Section

Reading	25 minutes on text 1 including reading time
	25 minutes on text 2 including reading time
	25 minutes on synthesis and comparison questions – texts 1 and 2
	5 minutes checking
Writing	45 minutes including planning and checking

Examiner tip
Do not use less than 45 minutes on the Writing section. Remember that it is worth 50% of this paper.

Examiner tip
Shorter questions may take you less time, which will leave some extra time for the longer questions.

Examiner tip
In the exam you must also annotate the questions; underline key words to keep your answer linked to the question focus.

Which techniques will help me to raise my grade?

This section of the textbook will outline techniques to help you do well. Activities focusing on each exam question type will be based on one or two text extracts. You must print these out before you begin work.

You will practice important techniques such as:

ANNOTATION
Before completing your answers, mark up text extracts by:
- Underlining key quotations.
- Boxing off sub-sections of text that are the focus of a particular question, using the line references given.
- Annotating specific language and structure techniques used by the writer to consider their effect for Question 3.
- Annotating aspects of:
    - Setting
    - Incidents/Issues
    - Themes
    - Events

to evaluate the writer's success in relation to the question focus for Question 6.

CHECKING YOUR WORK
You must keep a final 5 minutes to check your written work.

TIMING
Managing your time for each question will help you to be successful.

PLANNING TECHNIQUES
For synthesis, comparison and Writing responses.

153

Preparing for your exams

Paper 2 Questions 1 & 2

Assessment objectives
- To find information (part of AO1)

Texts
This section uses the source text *Letter from a journalist: The Aberfan Disaster* by Alix Palmer.

What is the examiner looking for?
Questions 1 and 2 focus on the first part of AO1: 'identify'. They test whether you can find information. You are not asked to interpret or analyse it. Just find the shortest quotation that fully answers the question and copy it out.

Question format
Questions 1 and 2 will always begin with the following words:

From lines [...], identify **two**....

Examiner tip

The use of quotation marks is not required for these questions.

The questions might ask you to find information about a person, thing, setting, action or event. Question 2 invites you to use your own words or quotations from the text. It is advisable to use direct quotations where possible.

Read the example questions below.

1 From lines 3–10, identify **two** items that Ada thinks will help make the evening memorable.

1 ....

2 ....

(Total for Question 1 = 2 marks)

2 From lines 1–5, identify **two** negative effects of the volcano on the landscape. You may use your own words or quotations from the text.

1 ....

2 ....

(Total for Question 2 = 2 marks)

Paper 2 Questions 1 & 2

Timing ⏱

You should allow 25 minutes to complete all of Questions 1, 2, and 3 which are on Text 1. You should find that Questions 1 and 2 require very little time. Before completing Questions 1 and 2, you should spend five minutes reading and understanding the first text extract.

| Text 1 | Questions 1, 2, 3 | 2, 2, 15 marks | 25 minutes including reading |

Check your answers and then move on quickly to save time for Question 3, which is worth more marks.

Key steps

Read and understand the passage. ▶ Underline the key words in the question – the line references and the focus you are looking for. ▶ Use your pen to box off the sub-extract defined by the question, using the line references at the side of the margin. ▶ Underline the two shortest relevant words or phrases in the source text that fully answer the question. ▶ Copy out each short quotation. Add your own words only if it is absolutely necessary.

Linked source text: *Letter from a journalist: The Aberfan Disaster* **by Alix Palmer**

The Aberfan disaster occurred in October 1966 in a Welsh mining village. The collapse of a colliery killed 116 children and 28 adults. This edited letter was written by journalist Alix Palmer, then aged 27. As well as completing her report on the disaster, she wrote to her mother about the horror she had witnessed.

Before considering the worked example and activities in this section, read and understand the full extract. Check the glossary for unfamiliar words.

155

Preparing for your exams

Worked example

> 1. From lines 2–6, identify **two** actions carried out by reporters (including the writer) on hearing the news of the disaster.

Candidate has annotated key words

| caught the midday train | had lunch |

The exact answers have been given. ✓

> Dear Mummy,
>
> You probably noticed that I was in Aberfan this weekend. But you will have no possible idea of what hell it was. No newspaper could ever paint a picture terrible enough.
>
> The first news reached the office at 11a.m., just that 50 children were trapped. I caught the midday train and met many other reporters from various newspapers also on it. We had lunch which was a good thing because it was a long time before we could eat again or even feel hungry.
>
> At Cardiff, the Express had hired cars waiting but we were told the only way to get through was by train. The roads were closed.

(5)

Building your skills

Activity 1

Questions 1 and 2 in the exam should be quick and straightforward. There are some common reasons why students do not gain full marks.

Look at the answers to Question 2, using another section of the source text *Letter from a journalist: The Aberfan Disaster*. Which would gain:

- full marks
- one mark
- no marks?

Rank the answers, giving reasons for the marks you give them, copying out the first and last columns of the table on the next page.

> 2. From lines 10–14, identify **two** factors which resulted in the village of Aberfan being crowded. You may use your own words or quotations from the text.

Candidate	Factor 1	Factor 2	Mark and feedback
Candidate A	There were a lot of people: 'many people in filthy clothes'	'There were miners coming from the pits'	
Candidate B	Women were standing in the road	The roads were closed	
Candidate C	Women lined the streets	lorries and ambulances blocked every inch	

Activity 2

1. Now apply these skills to answer an example exam-style question on the next section of Alix Palmer's letter. Refer to the Key steps on page 155 to help you.

> **Examiner tip**
>
> Remember to check that your given answer is from within the line references stated in the question.

> 1 From lines 15–23, identify **two** examples of why the writer believes no more people will be found alive in the school.

2. Read the final paragraph of the Aberfan letter and write your own Questions 1 or 2 for a partner to answer. You must know the potential answers to your questions before you ask a partner to complete them. Remember that Question 2 offers the option to 'use your own words'.

Preparing for your exams

Paper 2 Question 3

Assessment objectives

- Explain, comment on and analyse how writers use language and structure to achieve effects and influence readers, using relevant subject terminology to support their views (AO2)

Texts

This section uses the source texts *An Astronaut's Guide to Life on Earth* by Chris Hadfield and *Letter from a journalist: The Aberfan Disaster* by Alix Palmer.

What is the examiner looking for?

Question 3 is a longer answer question. As with the equivalent question on Paper 1, you must:

- identify the writer's choices of both language <u>and</u> structure. **Your marks will be limited if you do not consider both.**
- explain their effects on the reader. **This second aspect is very important and is the real focus of the question.**

You will focus on the **whole** of Text 1. Your points must:

- link to the focus of the question
- use textual references
- analyse their effect on the reader.

Question format

Question 3 will always be worded in this way:

> 3 Analyse how the writer uses language and structure to interest and engage the reader.
>
> In your answer you should write about:
>
> - language features and techniques
> - structural features and techniques
> - the effect on the reader.
>
> Support your views with detailed reference to the text.
>
> (Total for Question 3 = 15 marks)

Timing

Timing on Paper 2 is challenging. Leave enough time in your 25 minutes to spend most of it on Question 3.

| Text 1 | Questions 1, 2, 3 | 2, 2, 15 marks | 25 minutes including reading |

158

Paper 2 Question 3

Key steps

Identify the TAPS of the article to think carefully about how the text might 'interest and engage' the intended reader. ▶ Underline the key phrases in the question: 'language and structure' and 'interest and engage'. ▶ Annotate the extract. Mark language and structural features. Think about how they work to 'interest and engage'. ▶ Write your answer, using concise **P**oint, **E**vidence, **A**nalysis for at least 5 points.

Linked source text: *An Astronaut's Guide to Life on Earth* **by Chris Hadfield**

Before working through the activities, you should:

- read and understand the extract from Chris Hadfield's *An Astronauts' Guide to Life on Earth*
- identify the Text type, Audience, Purpose and Source of the extract.

Worked example

The example below shows the first paragraph annotations by a candidate. Notice which features of language and structure have been identified. Look at the notes on their effect.

> **3** Analyse how <u>the writer uses language and structure to interest and engage the reader</u>.
>
> In your answer you should write about:
>
> - language features and techniques
> - structural features and techniques
> - the effect on the reader.
>
> Support your views with detailed reference to the text.
>
> (Total for Question 3 = 15 marks)

Mission Impossible

The windows of a spaceship casually frame miracles. Every 92 minutes, another sunrise: a layer cake that starts with orange, then a thick wedge of blue, then the richest, darkest icing decorated with stars. The secret patterns of our planet are revealed: mountains bump up rudely from orderly plains, forests are green gashes edged with snow, rivers glint in the sunlight, twisting and turning like silvery worms. Continents splay themselves out whole, surrounded by islands sprinkled across the sea like delicate shards of shattered eggshells.

(5)

structure – moves from window to outside

metaphor – helps imagine picture

nouns – colour = visual

possessive pronoun – involves reader

alliteration – romantic picture

simile = visual picture

personification – spaceship and landscape as alive – vivid

simile = visual

Preparing for your exams

Activity 1

This question builds on the work you have done for Paper 1 Question 3. You have learned features of language and structure that you used for Paper 1. Some additional features are relevant for non-fiction.

1. Identify the features of language and structure below that you would usually find in non-fiction texts rather than fiction texts.

Language	Structure
Interesting choices of vocabulary	Title, headings, subheadings
Figurative language (simile, metaphor, personification)	Beginning, middle, end Introduction, main text, conclusion
Imagery/symbolism	Shifts in attitudes/viewpoints/topics
Word classes: nouns, verbs, adjectives, adverbs	Shifts at the beginning/middle/end of the text
Repetition of words (in close proximity)	'Zooming in' – moving from the general to the particular
Tone: words that establish formality/informality/humour/sarcasm/mood	'Zooming out' – moving from one example to the bigger picture
Rhetorical devices: use of 'you', imperatives/commands	Sets of 3, rhetorical questions
Facts and statistics	Repetition of words, phrases, ideas across the extract
Opinions	Punctuation, for example, question marks, ellipses, exclamations, pauses
Quotations, direct and indirect speech and references	Connectives – to show contrast or to build on one idea
Familiar references, anecdotes to illustrate, 'true life stories'	Sentence types (minor, simple, compound, complex)
Specialist language	Sentence lengths (short, long)

2. Look back at the opening paragraph of the extract. Can you add to the original annotations, identifying any other features? Use the table above to help you.

3. Annotate your printed copy of the text, thinking carefully about how each feature would interest and engage the reader.

Activity 2

For Paper 2 Language and structure, you are commenting on the construction of the **whole** text rather than a paragraph or two as you did for Paper 1.

Using your printout of the text, scan the whole extract to consider structure. Write your answers to the following questions:

- Where is Tim Hadfield at the beginning of the extract?
- Where is he at the end of the extract?
- Can you identify a shift or turning point in the extract, for example, a change in place, tone or attitude? Copy out the quotation and explain the reasons for your choice.

Question 3 tests your ability to explain the *effect* of language and structure in relation to the question focus. Time is short so your points must be precise and contain the following aspects:

- PEA (point, evidence, analysis)
- relevant quotations or line references
- identification of specific features used
- explanation of the effect of features in relation to the question
- use of literary terms.

Activity 3

1. Read the opening two paragraphs of the source text again and consider the first two points made by the candidate below. The first point is skilfully written.

    a. How would you improve point 2 (the second paragraph), below? Write down your advice to this student.

    b. Now redraft the paragraph to improve it.

    Candidate X

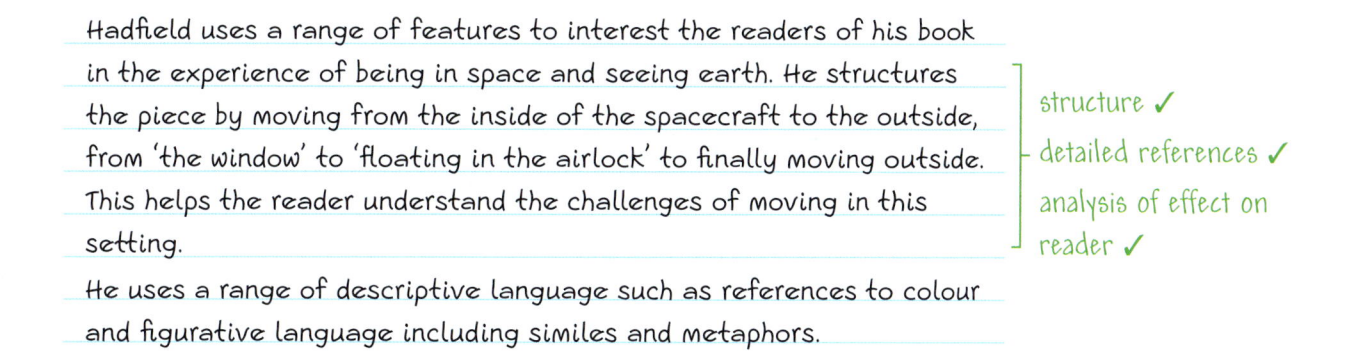

    > Hadfield uses a range of features to interest the readers of his book in the experience of being in space and seeing earth. He structures the piece by moving from the inside of the spacecraft to the outside, from 'the window' to 'floating in the airlock' to finally moving outside. This helps the reader understand the challenges of moving in this setting.
    >
    > He uses a range of descriptive language such as references to colour and figurative language including similes and metaphors.

    Annotations: structure ✓ / detailed references ✓ / analysis of effect on reader ✓

2. Write a third point, using the model of the first point above to help you. Focus your point on the writer's use of factual language. Check your answer against the success criteria below:

    - point identifying a specific feature of language and structure
    - evidence
    - analysis linking to the interest of the reader.

Preparing for your exams

Activity 4

1. Before you begin this writing activity, annotate the rest of the extract, to identify features of language and structure. Use the table on page 160 to help you.

   You can achieve full marks on this question by:
   - looking for features commonly found in most non-fiction texts
   - adding one or two points that stand out in the given extract.

   By following the checklist below, you will cover the aspects required for the mark scheme without needing to worry about whether a point covers language or structure.

   Question 3 full answer checklist

Points about:	Example features:	Effect on the reader:
Vocabulary	Descriptive language/specialist terminology/a range of adjectives/a range of place names	This interests the reader because…
Sentence lengths	A minor sentence/A long sentence/A short sentence	The effect of this is to engage the reader by…
Beginning/end/shift	Moves from inside to outside/changes the mood in paragraph 4/shifts to the opinions of others in the middle of the article	This sudden change will interest the reader since…
More PEA points on language/structure features that may interest and engage the reader		

   > **Examiner tip**
   >
   > Question 3 in Paper 2 requires a longer answer than the equivalent question in Paper 1. It carries more marks and is on the whole of the source text.

   > **Examiner tip**
   >
   > When time is short you can also try to use a quotation to make more than one point about language *and* structure. For example:
   >
   > He structures the piece by zooming out, from the inside of the spacecraft to the outside, from 'the window' to 'floating in the airlock'. This helps the reader understand the challenges of moving in this setting. The use of verbs such as 'floating' helps the reader understand more about the physical difficulties.

2. Now complete a full answer to the Question 3 on 'Mission Impossible'. Include the three analytical points already written by yourself and Candidate X (in Activity 3) and complete the full answer to address a range of points.

3. Look back at your answer. Check you have used subject terminology where appropriate.

   > **Examiner tip**
   >
   > Using terminology displays your knowledge of features of language and structure but it is of no value unless you also explain why the writer's use of features might be engaging.

Activity 5

Now apply these skills to answer the exam-style question below using the full text 'Letter from a Journalist: The Aberfan Disaster'. Use all the advice and checklists earlier in this unit to help you write a high quality answer.

Read the example question below.

> **3** Analyse how the writer uses language and structure to interest and engage the reader.
>
> In your answer you should write about:
> - language features and techniques
> - structural features and techniques
> - the effect on the reader.
>
> Support your views with detailed reference to the text.
>
> **(Total for Question 3 = 15 marks)**

Paper 2 Questions 4 & 5

Assessment objectives
- To interpret information (part of AO1)

Texts
This section uses the source text Review of 'Dans le Noir?' by Jasper Gerard.

What is the examiner looking for?

Questions 4 and 5 focus on AO1. They test whether you can find information, which might involve you interpreting* the text. These questions require a short answer, so avoid wasting time using too many words.

For Question 4, you can use your own words if necessary. However, try to lift a short quotation or piece of information directly from the text – when you use your own words instead, you can change the meaning of the text by mistake.

Question 5 requires you to find a quotation. You are not given the option to use your own words.

English term
Interpret: Read between the lines to come to a conclusion

Examiner tip
More successful candidates give brief and compact responses.

Preparing for your exams

Question format

Question 4 asks you to find information and may be worded:

> 4   From lines [...], identify....

You are being asked to find, and sometimes interpret, a relevant statement in the text.

Read the example questions below.

> 4   From lines 1–5, identify how employment rights for women have improved.
>
>   ....
>
>   ....
>
>   (Total for Question 4 = 1 mark)

Question 5 asks you to identify a phrase and will be worded:

> 5   In lines [...], identify a/the phrase which shows....

Some questions will have more than one possible answer, while others will ask you to find the only relevant phrase.

Read the example questions below.

> 5   In lines 14–18, identify the phrase which shows how the project was difficult.
>
>   ....
>
>   ....
>
>   (Total for Question 5 = 1 mark)

Timing

Before completing Questions 4 and 5, you should spend five minutes reading and understanding the second text extract.

| Text 2 | Questions 4, 5, 6 | 1, 1, 15 marks | 25 minutes including reading |

You should find that these straightforward questions take less time; they are only worth one mark each. Check your answers and then move on quickly, to save time. Within this 25 minute slot, Question 6 is worth far more marks and needs the most time.

Examiner tip

A range of answers is usually possible. These are short-answer questions so find the most straightforward answer.

Paper 2 Questions 4 & 5

Key steps

Read and understand the passage. ▶ Underline the question's key words, line references and the focus you are looking for. ▶ Use your pen to box off the sub-extract defined by the question, using the line references at the side of the margin. ▶ Underline the most relevant short phrase. ▶ Copy out the short quotation (for question 4 you might need to put it into your own words to make your interpretation clear).

Linked source text: Review of 'Dans le Noir?'

This restaurant review, written by a food critic for a national newspaper, focuses on an unusual restaurant where people eat in the dark.

Before considering the following worked example and activities, read and understand the full review. Check the glossary for unfamiliar words and use the surrounding text to make an intelligent guess for any others.

> **Examiner tip**
> Remember to identify the TAPS (see page 77) before working on any non-fiction text.

Worked example

4 From lines 1-5, identify why the meal took place.

....

(Total for Question 4 = 1 mark)

He was a dear friend and I hadn't clapped eyes on him in years. He was over from Los Angeles and wanted dinner that night. I had to eat at *Dans le Noir?** for the purpose of this review, so Diana and I asked him along. And there I sat chomping away with a mucker* I'd been longing to see – in the dark. (5)

The lobby is lit, but as we are ignored we wander through a curtain. Uh-oh. We are enveloped in blackness. Forget the Congo, this is the heart of darkness.

Glossary

Dans le Noir: In the dark (French)

Mucker: Friend

Candidate A	'for the purpose of this review'	The candidate uses a quotation. ✓
Candidate B	His friend was visiting and wanted to have dinner.	Interprets using own words. ✓
Candidate C	To meet both work and social needs simultaneously.	Interprets using own words. ✓

165

Preparing for your exams

Building your skills

Activity 1

These questions should be quick and straightforward. There are some common reasons why students do not gain full marks.

Look at the answers below to a question based on another section of the review.

> **5** From lines 12–20, identify a phrase which shows why the guests found the restaurant experience confusing.
>
> ....
>
> (Total for Question 5 = 1 mark)

Candidate	Answer	Feedback
Candidate A	'we are ignored' – there is no-one to show them what to do	
Candidate B	'We are enveloped in blackness. Forget the Congo, this is the heart of darkness.'	
Candidate C	They can't see anything.	
Candidate D	'Back in the lobby, we are instructed to order there.'	

Identify which of the following examiner comments (1–4) applies to each answer (A–D) in the table above.

1. The candidate has used their own words which is not what the question asks for.
2. The quotation is longer than is needed.
3. Correct quotation used. No need for additional comment.
4. Outside the correct text area.

Activity 2

If you use your own words for Question 4 rather than a quotation, it is possible to change the meaning of the original text by mistake. Look at the answers to the questions on the next page. The candidates have paraphrased the original text.

1. Read the sub-extract identified in the question again.
2. Mark or write out the most relevant quotation that informs the candidate answers. You may identify more than one if necessary.

166

Paper 2 Questions 4 & 5

3. Identify which of the candidate answers A–E below:

   a. offer an accurate interpretation of the original quotation **OR**

   b. have slightly changed the original meaning by mistake.

4. From lines 48–54, identify one reason the writer gives to explain why the restaurant fails to achieve its aim.

   (Total for Question 4 = 1 mark)

Candidate	Answer
A	The chef is not skilful enough.
B	The chef makes food that doesn't taste right.
C	The chef is not Heston Blumenthal.
D	Diners can't tell what food they are eating.
E	The chef is not able to make food that tempts the senses.

Activity 3

Use what you have learned to complete the range of Question 4 and 5 style tasks below.

4 From lines 76–83, identify one way the restaurant could be viewed as admirable.

   ....

4 From lines 79–83, identify why the writer is not impressed with the restaurant.

   ....

5 From lines 62–66, identify a phrase that shows the food is not good in the restaurant.

   ....

5 From lines 70–78, identify the phrase that shows why the friends need another meal.

   ....

167

Preparing for your exams

Paper 2 Question 6

Assessment objectives
- To evaluate texts critically and support this with appropriate textual references (AO4)

Texts
This section uses the source texts *Frank Stephens' speech* and *What is a House?* by Caitlin Moran.

What is the examiner looking for?
Question 6 requires a longer answer. It focuses on evaluating the **whole** extract. Evaluating means looking at the whole from a distance. You must judge the success of the text, focusing on an aspect the writer is trying to achieve. Your judgement should be supported by evidence. You do not need to analyse evidence in extended detail.

Examiner tip
Your focus is to appreciate the writer's skill. In Paper 2 you can consider both the achievements and possible weaknesses of the writer. Think about how well they have achieved their Purpose in relation to the Audience of the particular Text type you are reading.

Question format
Question 6 will be written in a similar form to this:

> 6 The writer attempts to engage the reader through [...]. Evaluate how successfully this is achieved. Support your views with detailed reference to the text.
>
> (Total for Question 6 = 15 marks)

Read the example question below.

> 6 In this extract, the writer attempts to engage the reader through the description of the elephant. Evaluate how successfully this is achieved. Support your views with detailed reference to the text.
>
> (Total for Question 6 = 15 marks)

Timing

| Text 2 | Questions 4, 5, 6 | 1, 1, 15 marks | 25 minutes including reading |

This is a longer answer question worth many marks. Make sure you leave enough time to complete it fully.

Key steps

Underline the key words in the question – particularly the key focus of your evaluation given in the question.

▶ Identify the Text type, Audience, Purpose and Source (TAPS) of the text. Be clear about the writer's intended audience and the effect the piece of writing is meant to have.

▶ Move **chronologically** through the source text, marking up whether the author focuses on setting, incidents/issues, themes or events in relation to the given focus. Highlight evidence.

▶ Decide on a short summary statement in response to the key focus in the question.

▼

Read your answer again and check you have used evaluative language.

◀ Write up your answer, beginning with a short summary statement and moving chronologically through the text to evaluate relevant aspects of SITE, using examples.

Activity 1

Identify the focus of each of the questions below, as practice for the exam. Write out the key words to record your answers.

> **Examiner tip**
> Candidates should focus on what the question asks them to evaluate, not just on evaluating 'the text'.

6 In this extract, there is an attempt to be critical of the managers of the factory. Evaluate how successfully this is achieved. Support your views with detailed reference to the text.

(Total for Question 6 = 15 marks)

6 In this extract, the writer tries to engage the reader through the description of his relationship with the local people. Evaluate how successfully this is achieved. Support your views with detailed reference to the text.

(Total for Question 6 = 15 marks)

Linked source text: *Frank Stephens' speech*

Frank Stephens is a man with Down syndrome. In 2016 he gave a famous speech in the American Congress about how attitudes towards the syndrome, and research linked to it, should be more positive.

Before you begin, remind yourself of the aspects of evaluating a text. On page 69, you learned how to consider Settings, Ideas and Incidents, Themes, and Events (SITE) as a method of assessing how the writer has attempted to show something. This method links directly to the way the examiners mark this question.

Preparing for your exams

The aspect of **Setting** for non-fiction texts is slightly different from Paper 1 fiction texts. It can be helpful to check the relevance of the following:

- Is a specific place described?
- Is there a particular time, event or situation that provides a background to the text?
- Are there particular views or circumstances that the writer is responding to?
- Is there a particular intended audience/reader from a specific place/time?

Activity 2

Look back at some of the texts already addressed in this book. Identify which aspects of setting anchor each one. The first example is done for you.

Text	Setting: date, place, situation, reader, audience
Letter from a journalist: The Aberfan Disaster	Date: 1966 writing date Place: Welsh mining town setting Situation: a professional daughter writing to her mother Reader/Audience: the mother
An Astronaut's Guide to Life on Earth	
Dans Le Noir? review	

Activity 3

Read Frank Stephens' speech. You will need to be familiar with the content to complete the following activities.

1. Identify the Text type, Audience, Purpose and Source. Then focus on the exam-style question below.

   > 6 Frank Stephens attempts to engage the audience by showing that efforts to eliminate Down syndrome are wrong. Evaluate how successfully this is achieved. Support your views with detailed reference to the text.
   >
   > **(Total for Question 6 = 15 marks)**

2. Write out the question and underline the key words. Make sure you have identified the key focus of the question. Any aspects of SITE that you identify should be linked to this.

Activity 4

In Unit 6.3, for prose fiction the exam approach for evaluation considered **Ideas** or **Incidents** using the SITE/TIES method. This method is also relevant for evaluating non-fiction. Depending on the text type, ideas or incidents may be more relevant.

For example, in *The Aberfan Disaster*, **ideas** to do with the separation between reporters and locals are important. **Incidents** such as the closure of the roads are also relevant.

In the speech you have just read, **ideas** are more important. The speaker refers to important medical, political and social issues in his speech to Congress. He uses these to show that attempts to eliminate Down syndrome are wrong.

Read through the extracts below.

Extract	Idea
Just so there is no confusion, let me say that I am not a research scientist. However, no one knows more about life with Down syndrome than I do. Whatever you learn today, please remember this: I am a man with Down syndrome and my life is worth living.	He enjoys his own life.
It's **hard** for me to sit here and say those words. I completely understand that the people pushing this particular 'final solution' are saying that people like me should not exist. That view is deeply prejudiced by an outdated idea of life with Down syndrome.	People who think Down syndrome should be eliminated have prejudiced and old-fashioned ideas.

Now track through the rest of the speech to identify further ideas and issues that the speaker raises to show that attempts to eliminate Down syndrome are wrong.

Activity 5

A theme is a key idea that runs throughout a text, such as love, power, violence, the supernatural, and death. A theme is often reflected in the vocabulary that is used within the text: you will see a network of words that link to it.

In the exam you do not need to be overly concerned with separating themes and ideas. You will gain credit for mentioning relevant aspects and judging them in relation to the question focus.

1. Look at the list of possible themes below. Discuss them with a partner. Select three themes from the list that you agree are most relevant to this speech and the question focus. Remember, there is no one correct answer.

   > 6. Frank Stephens attempts to engage the audience by showing that attempts to eliminate Down syndrome are wrong. Evaluate how successfully this is achieved. Support your views with detailed reference to the text.
   >
   > (Total for Question 6 = 15 marks)

   Medical research   Science   Poverty   History   Money   Death

   Success   Life   Quality of life   Ethics   Power   Greed   Religion

Preparing for your exams

2. Using your printout of the speech, annotate the text where each of the themes you have chosen is most relevant, as you did on page 139.

Worked example

Activity 6

Remind yourself of the question focus on this text.

Responding to Paper 1 Question 6 requires you to do two key things:

- Annotate the text clearly to identify aspects of SITE.
- Write this up as a longer answer.

1. Read through the student response below. Notice how the annotations on the source text reflect the content of the answer.

> **Examiner tip**
> Various themes can be identified within any text. There is often more than one way of referring to each theme. One student may identify 'power', another 'status'. Both these terms are versions of the same idea, so are equally correct.

> **Examiner tip**
> You do not need to write about every paragraph of the text if you have not found something relevant to the question focus in a particular section.

Mr. Chairman and members of the committee,

Just so there is no confusion, let me say that I am not a research scientist. However, no one knows more about life with Down syndrome than I do. Whatever you learn today, please remember this: I am a man with Down syndrome and my life is worth living.

S**I**TE — The setting of Congress and the man delivering the speech having Down syndrome is powerful

S**I**TE — Idea of pleasure

(5)

Sadly, across the world, a notion is being sold that maybe we don't need research concerning Down syndrome. Some people say prenatal screens will identify Down syndrome in the womb and those pregnancies will just be terminated.

SI**T**E — Theme of medical research and eugenics

It's **hard** for me to sit here and say those words.

(10)

I completely understand that the people pushing this particular 'final solution' are saying that people like me should not exist. That view is deeply prejudiced by an outdated idea of life with Down syndrome.

S**I**TE — Idea of outdated attitudes

SITE — Setting of 21st century America

I have lectured at universities, acted in an award-winning film and an Emmy-winning TV show, and spoken to thousands of young people about the value of inclusion in making America great. I have been to the White House twice – and I didn't have to jump the fence either time.

(15)

S**I**TE — Theme of success and greatness. Idea of happiness and quality of life.

172

Overall in this extract the speaker successfully encourages his audience to understand more about the value of life with Down syndrome and that people who want to eliminate it are wrong.

The opening emphasises the idea of personal experience and he uses this to effectively convey his views. The setting of Congress would be important here since his physical presence on delivering this speech would have an impact on the people actually listening. He talks about the fact that some people believe he shouldn't exist: 'my life is worth living'. He is living evidence that the views of those people are wrong.

The idea of outdated attitudes in line 13 works well as the speaker reminds listeners of the setting of the twenty-first century. This works well to emphasise his view that people like this are wrong. The details he gives in the next paragraph ('lectured at universities, acted in an award-winning film') prove this and he powerfully develops the theme of success and quality of life that run through the speech. Perhaps it could have been more effective to balance these with more everyday points, rather than just extraordinary, since many people without Down syndrome will not have done such things themselves.

2. Write a list of the evaluative words and phrases the student has used. Remember to use these words in your own writing.

3. Identify the phrases in the student example that show she is keeping to the question focus: 'by showing that attempts to eliminate Down syndrome are wrong'.

Activity 7

1. Complete the annotations for the rest of the speech using your own printout of the text.
2. Now write the second half of this evaluation, in line with the question.

- Keep to the question focus: 'by showing that attempts to eliminate Down syndrome are wrong'.
- Use evaluative language to make a judgement, focusing on what is good, but perhaps suggesting an aspect you think could be better.
- Use short embedded quotations.
- Consider all aspects of SITE but remember you only need to write about the most significant aspects.
- Add a final brief section commenting on textual evidence. Explain techniques such as language and structure that add to the effectiveness of the speech. Link clearly to the question focus.

Use the sentence starters below to help you:

- Overall the language of this speech…
- The structure of the speech works well…

Preparing for your exams

Activity 8

Linked source text: 'What is a House?' by Caitlin Moran

Now apply all these skills to your own evaluation of another non-fiction extract. In the exam, this will be an extract you have already read, to complete earlier questions on AO1 and AO2.

Read the passage 'What is a House?' by Caitlin Moran and write your answer to the question below. Spend five minutes reading the extract before you begin.

> **6** The writer attempts to engage the reader through the description of her childhood home. Evaluate how successfully this is achieved.
>
> (Total for Question 6 = 15 marks)

You will need to use a printout of the text.

Remember to:

Read and understand the passage.	▶	Identify the TAPS.	▶	Annotate the question and the sections of the text using SITE, keeping the question focus in mind.
End with a brief overall comment about language and structure.	◀	Use evaluative language.	◀	Write up your answer, beginning with an opening summary statement and moving chronologically through the text to evaluate SITE using examples. Refer back to the question focus regularly.

Paper 2 Question 7a

Assessment objectives

- To select and synthesise evidence from different texts (part of AO1)

Texts

This section uses the following pairs of source texts:

- *An Astronaut's Guide to Life on Earth* by Chris Hadfield and 'On the moon after perfect touchdown' by Anthony Tucker

For this question, you will consider two non-fiction texts. One will be literary non-fiction and one will be non-fiction, such as a magazine or newspaper article.

Paper 2 Question 7a

What is the examiner looking for?
Question 7a focuses on the second part of AO1. You must synthesise (combine) information from two different texts into your own written answer, using relevant textual evidence to support your statements.

Question format
Question 7a will begin with the following words:

> **7 a** The two texts show […]. What similarities do the […] share in these extracts?
>
> (Total for Question 7a = 6 marks)

The question will always ask about similarities. The first sentence of the question will just establish a link between the two texts; it does not state the focus for your reading. Question 7a does **not** ask you to compare texts. You are being asked to combine basic information selected from the two texts. You are not being asked to unpick complex ideas or viewpoints. You are not being asked to analyse the text or focus on how it is written.

Read the example question below.

> **7 a** The two texts show some of the problems that happen in families. What similarities do the families share in these extracts?
>
> ....
>
> ....
>
> (Total for Question 7a = 6 marks)

Examiner tip
Notice the difference between the first and second sentences in the question. The first gives an overview of the subject of the extract. The second is the focus of your work.

Examiner tip
It is important to include a *range* of relevant points with evidence, linked to the question focus. For most students, 3 to 4 points is enough. Question 7b requires a longer answer so leave enough time for that.

Timing
You will have read both source texts during the first two sections of the exam in order to have completed Questions 1 to 6. Now in Questions 7a and 7b you will work on both texts together. Before you work on the two texts together.

The rough guide to timing for the questions on both texts is:

| Question 7a and 7b | 6, 14 marks | Synthesis and comparison | 25 minutes including reading |

Questions 7a and 7b are both high mark questions. By this point in the paper it is essential that you have 25 minutes of your Section A time left plus 5 minutes checking time.

175

Preparing for your exams

Key steps

| Underline the question's key words and the focus for the synthesis. | Skim read both texts to identify the main points of connection in relation to the question focus. | Draw out a quick plan to identify the ways both texts connect (see example below). | Annotate each text to reflect the numbered points in your plan. | Write up your synthesis, establishing an overall point and then linking both texts, and providing evidence through short quotations. |

Worked example: annotation and planning

The example below draws on two short texts. In the exam, Question 7a will focus on two longer texts which will total around 1000 lines.

You must spend a few minutes annotating and planning your answer to achieve your synthesis. The process below outlines the steps for answering Question 7a:

a. Identify the links between the texts linked to the question focus, drawing a brief numbered plan.

b. Find and mark up relevant quotations in each text, using the numbers from your plan.

c. Write up your answer using the points and evidence to link both texts to the question focus.

> **7 a** The two texts show the experiences of journeys. <u>What similarities do the travellers share</u> in these extracts?
>
> (Total for Question 7a = 6 marks)

i) Plan: identifying the links between the texts

PLAN	SIMILARITIES
1	unexpected events
2	difficult
3	lots of walking
4	obstructed/blocked

ii) Annotations

Use the numbers in your plan to mark the points of similarity between the texts to save time.

Paper 2 Question 7a

Text 1

The Aberfan Disaster

I caught the midday train and met many other reporters from various newspapers also on it. (5) We had lunch which was a good thing because it was a long time before we could eat again or even feel hungry.

At Cardiff, the Express had hired cars waiting but we were told the only way to get through was by train. The roads were closed. Even then we assumed they were closed because the "landslide" had descended on them. We still didn't know what had really happened. (10)

We left the train at Merthyr Vale, the village before Aberfan, about two miles away, and walked. The roads were just like they were during the war, with many people in filthy clothes all plodding in the same direction. These were the miners coming from the pits to join in the digging. In the village itself, women lined the streets and lorries and ambulances blocked every inch of the way. I think then we realised it was more serious than had first appeared (15) on the news tapes.

Text 2

Walking the Himalayas

'Very easy, two hours.' He smiled. It was a natural, innocent smile, and I was determined to trust him.

'Okay,' I said. It was either that or slip back into my routine of waiting for the heavens to open from my cheap hotel. And after the drama of the riot I didn't want to risk being stuck (5) inside again. So we walked. And walked, and walked. At the beginning it was in silence as I struggled to keep pace and catch my breath. The trail wound through the rhododendron bushes and monsoon forest, often disappearing into the tangled vines that battled to suffocate man's pitiful interference. I enjoyed the feeling of putting one foot in front of the other, of leaving the concrete and dust behind. (10)

Examiner tip

Note that the most important guidance in this question is the **second statement**. The first statement merely tells you what the two texts are about; it is not the focus of your work on synthesis.

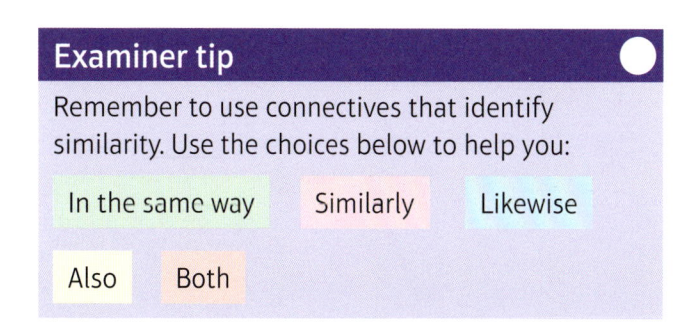

Examiner tip

Remember to use connectives that identify similarity. Use the choices below to help you:

In the same way   Similarly   Likewise

Also   Both

Preparing for your exams

Activity 1

1. Read through the first two points from a good student answer, based on the plan on page 176.

2. Develop the answer by adding the final two points about the texts on page 177, using the plan and annotations. Remember that you are not analysing the effects of writers' choices. You are just selecting points of connection and combining them, using quotations to prove your points.

> **7 a** The two texts show the experiences of journeys. <u>What similarities do the travellers share</u> in these extracts?
>
> (Total for Question 7a = 6 marks)

Examiner tip

Question 7a should be straightforward. The reasons students under-perform on this question are:
a) not planning in relation to the question focus
b) not annotating, to select short relevant quotations
c) wasting time on language analysis – AO2 is not assessed for this question
d) not leaving enough time for this question.

Candidate answer

Both travellers appear to find their journeys marked by unexpected events. The journalist in Text 1 arrives to find that despite the prearranged taxis, they are unable to use them ('closed the roads') and the traveller in text 2 is told that the journey will be 'Very easy, two hours', only to find this is not the case. In addition, the journeys both turn out to be difficult since Text 1 mentions the lengthy distance 'two miles away' and Text 2 also states 'I struggled'.

Annotations:
- relevant point of connection
- makes it clear which text is in focus using text 1/2
- link to text 1
- short relevant quotation
- connective
- short relevant quotation
- connective of similarity
- second point of connection
- connective of similarity
- relevant quotation which demonstrates the candidate's skills of inference

Activity 2

Linked source texts: *An Astronaut's Guide to Life on Earth* by Chris Hadfield and 'On the moon after perfect touchdown', by Anthony Tucker

Before working on the following activities, read both source texts. In the exam you will have already read them to complete questions 1–6.

Before you begin work on the two Space extracts in relation to an exam-style question:

1. Read and annotate the question below.

   > **7 a** The two texts show the experiences of being in space. What similarities do the spacemen share in these extracts?
   >
   > **(Total for Question 7a = 6 marks)**

2. Following the example of the plan on page 176, complete your own plan identifying the points of similarity.

3. Use your printouts of both texts to annotate quotations using the numbers from your plan.

Activity 3

Now write your answer to the sample Question 7a. Use your plan from Activity 2 to support your writing.

PLAN	SIMILARITIES
1	
2	
3	
4	

Preparing for your exams

Paper 2 Question 7b

Assessment objectives
- Compare writers' ideas and perspectives as well as how these are conveyed (AO3)

Texts
This section uses the following pairs of source texts:
- *Shooting an Elephant* by George Orwell and 'Ivory is not beautiful, it's barbaric' by Nicky Campbell
- *An Astronaut's Guide to Life on Earth* by Chris Hadfield and 'On the moon after perfect touchdown' by Anthony Tucker.

What is the examiner looking for?
This question asks you to:
- compare* writers' ideas* and perspectives*
- select relevant quotations
- analyse the effect of language, structure or themes to comment on the writers' methods.

You will compare the two non-fiction texts you have already read earlier in the exam and which were used in Question 7a.

English term
*Compare: Identify similarities and differences

*Ideas: Points the writer makes about the topic

*Perspectives: The writer's views about the topic

Examiner tip
When answering this question you should consider 'what' *and* 'how'. You are comparing:
- **what** ideas and views are expressed in each text, with evidence

and then
- **how** the writer has used a range of language, structure or themes to develop this.

Question format
Read the example question below.

> **7 b** Compare how the writers of Text 1 and Text 2 present their ideas and perspectives about challenging experiences. Support your answer with detailed references to the texts.
>
> You should write about:
> - the ideas* and perspectives* of the writers
> - how they are presented
> - how they are similar/different.
>
> (Total for Question 7b = 14 marks)

180

Paper 2 Question 7b

> **Timing** 🕐
>
> You will have read both source texts during the first two sections of the exam, before you work on the two texts together.
>
> The rough guide to timing for all the questions on both texts is:
>
> | Synthesis and comparison | Question 7a and 7b | 6, 14 marks | 25 minutes including reading |
>
> Questions 7a and 7b are worth many marks. By this point in the paper it is essential that you have 25 minutes of your Section A time left. Question 7b is worth 14 marks. You must write an extended answer, identifying a range of points that cover both texts. Annotate both texts and make a clear plan before writing.

> **Examiner tip**
>
> The mark scheme for Question 7b indicates that 'Responses that are unbalanced will not be able to access Level 3 or above'. Try to deal with both texts roughly equally.

Key steps

Underline the question's key words and the focus for the comparison. ▶ Skim read both texts to identify the main points of comparison in relation to the question focus. ▶ Draw out a plan listing similarities and differences between the two texts (see example below). ▶ Underline relevant quotations in each source text. Annotate theme, language and structure. ▶ Write up your comparison.

Worked example: planning

Linked source texts: 'Ivory is not beautiful, it's barbaric' by Nicky Campbell and *Shooting an Elephant* by George Orwell.

Read both texts and ensure you have a printout of each to work from, before you complete the activities.

> **7 b** Compare how the writers of Text 1 and Text 2 present their ideas and perspectives about wild elephants. Support your answer with detailed references to the texts.

Worked example: planning

You must spend time annotating and planning your answer if you are to achieve a good mark. The process below shows you how to complete Question 7b.

a. Identify the similarities and differences between the two texts in line with the question focus.

b. Find and mark up relevant quotations in each text, annotating language, structure and theme.

c. Write up your answer using the points and evidence to link both texts to the question focus.

Preparing for your exams

Plan: identifying similarities and differences

Texts 1 and 2 Links – ideas and perspectives about elephants	Text 1 Ivory	Text 2 Elephant
Similarities established		
1. Their fate is controlled by humans		
2. Treated barbarically		
3.		
Differences established		
1. Beliefs about humans' control over animals		
2. Views towards other races about their attitudes towards elephants		
3.		

Activity 1

Read the plan, then copy it and add another point of similarity and another point of difference in column 1.

Worked example: annotation

Once you have identified several points of similarity and difference, you must underline relevant quotations. Annotate these to comment on the writer's craft, thinking about language, structure and theme.

Examiner tip

There will be a number of similarities/differences in ideas and attitudes in each passage. There is no single right answer; you must select a range of points and support them with quotations.

Examiner tip

Aim to make a range of points supported by quotations from **both** texts.

The example below shows the linked annotations on each text proving Similarity 1: 'both writers suggest that elephants' fate is controlled by humans'.

We have learned a lot about these extraordinary intelligent animals since King Leopold of the Belgians <u>mutilated his way through the great herds of the Congo</u>. Elephants mourn, they weep and they show empathy. This is not Disney. It's science. — language – aggressive king

It was perfectly clear to me what I <u>ought to do. I ought</u> to walk up to within, say, twenty-five yards of the elephant and test his behaviour. — language – repetition of ought – humans controlling the wild

182

Paper 2 Question 7b

Texts 1 and 2 Links – ideas and perspectives about elephants	Text 1 Ivory	Text 2 Elephant
Similarities established		
1. Their fate is controlled by humans	Writer believes humans have negatively affected elephants across history.	Writer believes his role is to control the wild animal.
2. Treated barbarically		
3.		
Differences established		
1. Beliefs about humans' control over animals		
2. Views towards other races about their attitudes towards elephants		
3.		

Activity 2

1. Now mark up relevant quotations on your printouts of the texts to illustrate the similarities and differences in your table. Use the example on the previous page to guide you.

2. Add annotations to consider the effect of language, structure and theme in relation to the exam question.

3. Complete columns 2 and 3 of your plan to summarise the specific points of similarity and difference in views and attitudes.

Examiner tip

In your written answer, quotations/references should be followed by explanation. Choose from the following phrases:

This suggests…   This implies…   From this, the reader can infer…

Examiner tip

Remember to use connectives that identify similarity and difference to move between the evidence relating to each text. Use the choices below to help you:

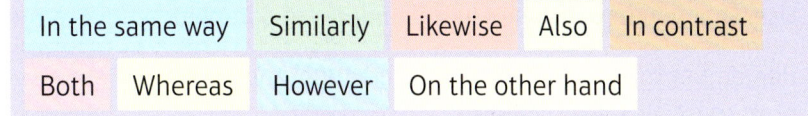

In the same way   Similarly   Likewise   Also   In contrast
Both   Whereas   However   On the other hand

Comparative points should follow the pattern below for each paragraph. Use this structure for each comparative point you make.

- Point of similarity/difference in relation to the question focus
- Text 1: Evidence plus analysis of idea/perspective
- Text 2: Evidence plus analysis of idea/perspective

Read the candidate answer on page 184 and note how the structure described above has been used for point one of the plan.

183

Preparing for your exams

| 1. Their fate is controlled by humans | Writer believes humans have negatively affected elephants across history | Writer believes his role is to control the wild animal |

Candidate answer

Both writers convey the perspective that elephants' fate is controlled by humans. Campbell cites a Belgian king who 'mutilated his way through the great herds of the Congo' showing that humans have affected elephants across history as well as today. Similarly Orwell seems to feel that the fate of the elephant is his responsibility, saying 'it was perfectly clear to me what I ought to do' with the word ought emphasising that control of animals and people is his official role in Burma.

- clear point of comparison and link to the question focus ✓
- uses writer's name to make text 1 reference clear ✓
- evidence followed by analysis ✓
- appropriate connective to link points of comparison ✓
- uses writer's name to make it clear which text is in focus ✓
- language analysis ✓

Activity 3

1. Now complete the remainder of this Question 7b answer, using the two other points of similarity and the three points of difference from the plan on page 182. Use the paragraph model on the previous page to help you.

2. Check your work.

   - Is each point relevant to the question focus?
   - Have you addressed both texts in each point?
   - Have you covered a range of points?
   - Does each point have evidence from each text?
   - Have you analysed the quotations, focusing on language, structure or theme?
   - Have you used connectives to establish similarity and difference?

> **Examiner tip**
>
> Aim to include a wide range of comparisons between the texts, analysing the writers' ideas and perspectives. Consider theme, language and/or structure.

Activity 4

Use what you have learned in this chapter to complete a full exam-style Question 7b without support.

Remember to apply the planning and annotation methods before you begin writing. You will need printouts of both source texts.

Linked source texts: *An Astronaut's Guide to Life on Earth* and 'On the moon after perfect touchdown'

> **7 b** Compare how the writers of Text 1 and Text 2 present their ideas and perspectives about the challenges of being in space. Support your answer with detailed references to the texts.
>
> You should write about:
>
> - the ideas and perspectives of the writers
> - how they are presented
> - how they are similar/different.
>
> (Total for Question 7b = 14 marks)

184

Paper 2 Questions 8 and 9

Assessment objectives

- Communication and organisation techniques (AO5)
- Vocabulary, sentence structure, SPaG (AO6)

What is the examiner looking for?

Questions 8 and 9 assess your ability to write clearly for a set purpose and audience. You only need to answer one question: *either* Question 8 *or* Question 9.

You could be asked to write a:

- newspaper article
- review
- leaflet
- text book entry
- speech
- letter

Examiner tip

When answering Question 8 or 9, the examiner will be looking for:

- clear focus on the purpose and audience of the text
- evidence that you have planned structure and content in your piece of writing
- accurate and appropriate vocabulary, spelling, punctuation and grammar.

Question format

Questions 8 and 9 will always ask you to write a particular text type. The questions may specify a particular audience.

There will be some bullet points which you can use as support for content and structure.

EITHER

8   Write a section of a history textbook about someone in history you consider to be a role model.

In your section, you could consider:

- who your role model is
- why you admire them
- why it is important to have role models

as well as any other ideas you might have.

Your response will be marked for the accurate and appropriate use of vocabulary, spelling, punctuation and grammar.

....

....

(Total for Question 8 = 40 marks)

Preparing for your exams

OR

9 Write a letter to a school newspaper to help raise money to build a new sports hall.

In your letter, you could consider:

- the reasons why a new sport hall is important
- how you plan to raise the money
- the facilities you would have in the hall

as well as any other ideas you might have.

Your response will be marked for the accurate and appropriate use of vocabulary, spelling, punctuation and grammar.

....

....

(Total for Question 8 = 40 marks)

Timing

Before completing Question 8 or 9, you should spend 5–10 minutes writing a plan. You will then have 30–35 minutes to write your response and 5 minutes to check your work at the end.

You have 45 minutes in total. Make sure you have left enough time to complete this question and aim to finish it in 40 minutes.

Key steps

Read both questions carefully. Underline the key words in each question before you decide which question you are going to answer. Check you have identified the Text type, Audience and Purpose of each question.

Consider various ideas before selecting the one you think will work best.

Spend 5–10 minutes planning your work. Be clear about how you are going to start and end your piece of work.

Use your plan as a guide to help structure your writing.

Check your response and correct any spelling, punctuation or grammar errors you might have made. (5 minutes)

Paper 2 Questions 8 & 9

Activity 1

1. Look at the task below. Which key words would you underline to help you plan your responses?
2. Copy the table and the second column, outlining the text type, audience and purpose of each question.

Question	
You have been asked to talk to a group of parents about social media. Write a speech outlining the benefits and dangers of social media for young people. In your speech, you could include: • why social media is important • how social media can be dangerous • suggestions around how to use it safely as well as any other ideas you might have.	Text type: Audience: Purpose:

Planning your work

It is really important to write a plan **before** you start writing. Make sure you label or number your plan to order your paragraphs. You may also wish to include ideas on appropriate language devices you might use.

Look at the example below.

Text type *purpose*

Write a (newspaper article) (explaining) why it is important to use less plastic.

Audience = newspaper readers

Tone = Formal

Headline: "STOP USING PLASTIC FOR THE GOOD OF THE PLANET"

Paragraph 1. Open with the arguments. Rhetorical question: What was the last piece of plastic you used?	P1: Suggests tone of the piece.
P2. Issue we are facing - 8 million tonnes thrown away each year.	P2: Use of statistics and examples.
P3. Plastics and the oceans. Damage to birds, fish and us.	
P4. Call to action - cut down on plastic.	
P5. Call to action - help clean up the damage.	
P6. Finish with the piece of plastic from the beginning. If you must use plastic, think about where that single piece will end up and ask yourself, do I really need this?	P6: Begins and ends with a question. Comes to a definite conclusion.

Preparing for your exams

Activity 2

Look again at the question in Activity 1 and write your own plan. Use the table below to help you.

Paragraph 1.
Paragraph 2.
Paragraph 3.
Paragraph 4.
Paragraph 5.
Paragraph 6.

Examiner tip

Failure to plan properly can have a big impact on your overall mark.

Articles and reviews

You will have practised writing a newspaper article in Unit 9. In the Paper 2 exam, you may be asked to write a newspaper article, magazine article or review. It is likely that the question will ask you to express a view on an issue which has been discussed in the texts you will have read for Section A.

An **article**:
- is usually found in a newspaper or a magazine
- is intended to inform the reader and/or persuade them of a particular point of view
- can offer one opinion or both sides of an argument.

A **review**:
- is usually found in a newspaper or a magazine
- presents the writer's opinion about the focus of the review such as a book, event, product, film, play or video game
- can be positive, negative or a mixture of the two.

Here are examples of an article and a review written by students in the exam.

> Write a newspaper article expressing your views about streaming music from the internet.

Start with a headline or something to grab the reader's attention

CAN YOU PUT A PRICE ON MUSIC?

Why it is important that we give musicians the financial recognition they deserve.

A sub-headline can help the reader see the line of argument the article will take.

Musicians are geniuses. They make us feel emotions and help us through the good and the bad times with their lyrics and their music. So why are so many people reluctant to pay for music these days? Is it theft or are we entitled to access this for free? In an internet age where almost everything can be found at the click of a mouse, this is an increasingly difficult question to answer.

This student has started with a short sentence and used a formal tone.

Question which is answered later in the piece.

9 out of 10 of us admit to downloading or streaming music for free but only 6 out of 10 of us think that this is stealing.

Statistics help to back up the argument.

> Write a review about an event you have attended.

NEW YEAR'S EVE SPECTACULAR!

London Fireworks display, 31 December

The firework display on New Year's Eve in London is crowded and cold – but it's the experience of a lifetime!

A positive headline lets the reader know that the writer enjoyed the experience.

informative strapline establishes 'what' and 'when'

A negative start with a short sentence to set the mood.

The crowd were uneasy and a little bit bored. It was 11:15 and midnight seemed a long way off. However, once we heard the first chime of midnight from Big Ben that was all forgotten as we were treated to a 15 minute display of lights against the backdrop of amazing landmarks.

Reviewer rating: 10/10

Clear conclusion using a common feature of reviews: a rating.

Preparing for your exams

Activity 3

1. Read the two short student answers on page 187 again and think about the similarities and differences between the two texts. Note down up to three of each and discuss them with a partner.

2. Write a review of an event you did not enjoy, and compare the tone, vocabulary and structure with the reviews on the previous page. Make careful use of tone and vocabulary so that the review is realistic and engaging.

Textbook sections and information leaflets

Textbook sections and information leaflets focus on giving information or conveying instructions. Information texts are not as personal as other types of writing, as you are not trying to persuade anyone to agree or disagree with your arguments. You do need to think about the tone of your piece and try to make it factual and objective.

Sections from textbooks and leaflets often organise information using:

- headings and sub-headings
- bullets
- numbered lists.

> **Examiner tip**
>
> The examiner is not testing you on the factual accuracy of the information in your writing. It is all about **how** you write your piece, the tone you maintain and the vocabulary you use to support the information you are giving.

Activity 4

1. In pairs, identify the key features of textbook extracts. Consider layout, tone and language style.

2. Write an introductory section for a textbook on healthy living for young people. In your section, you could include ideas about:

   - diet
   - exercise
   - balancing work and pleasure.

Activity 5

1. Look at each of the following extracts, taken from sample student answers to a similar task, and underline the key features of a textbook. Note what each candidate has missed out and think about how you would improve the pieces. Give three suggestions.

2. Look at the language used in both pieces. Underline the words that show the tone is objective or factual. Are there any words that are too personal? Select one of the pieces and suggest three changes to language that would improve the piece.

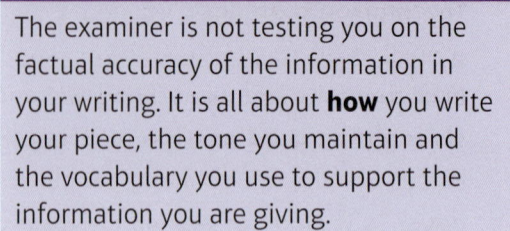

GETTING YOUR LIFE IN ORDER: EASY STEPS TO FOLLOW

To make your life better you need to think about what you do every day and change it. You should get up at the same time every day and make sure you know what you are going to wear and have everything you need ready in your bag for the rest of the day. I plan my meals in advance and go to the gym even though I hate it!

There are many ways that you can get your life in order. Taking it one step at a time works for a number of people. In this section of the book, we look at how small changes can make all the difference to your well-being as well as making the most of your day without feeling rushed or stressed. I would recommend these three key steps.

Top 3 ways you can manage your life:

1) Work. Think about what you need for work or school and make sure you have everything prepared from notes for a meeting all the way through to the books you need to read or take with you.

2) Health. Plan your meals and make packed lunches the night before. This will stop you snacking and will save time if you are busy all day.

3) Keep a diary. Know in advance what you are doing and schedule in your gym classes, music lessons and other appointments so you don't feel rushed getting to them.

Letter writing: the basics

You must know how to write a formal and informal letter before taking your GCSE English Language exam. Look back at Unit 9.3 to help you with this section.

The basic rules of writing a letter stay the same regardless of audience and purpose.

Openings

- Establish your purpose and audience.
- Remember to use formal language.
- Use the correct salutation: *Dear Sir/Madam* if you do not know their name, or *Dear Isabel*, for example, if you do know their name.

Main part of the letter

- Structure your letter in paragraphs. Each one should have a clear topic.
- Don't repeat yourself! Plan carefully.

> **Examiner tip**
>
> The examiner is marking the content of the letter, not the layout. Don't worry about addresses or date. However, you do need to start and end your letter correctly.

Preparing for your exams

Endings

- End your letter with a decisive statement or a clear indication of what you would like your recipient to do or feel.
- Remember to sign off your letter with either *Yours faithfully* if you have opened with *Dear Sir/Madam*, or *Yours sincerely* if you have used their name.

Activity 6

The table on the following page shows three examples of openings to student answers to the following exam-style question.

> Write a letter to your local Member of Parliament expressing your concerns about the recent proposals to build flats on the local park.

1. Read the three example answers.
2. Identify and write down one positive aspect of each answer.

Example
Candidate A: Dear Ms Lewis, I am writing to you today to express my extreme concern about the plans to build a 10 storey block of flats on the local park. My three main concerns surrounding these proposals are outlined below. Firstly, I am concerned that this building is being constructed on a park which is an area where the whole community are able to experience wildlife and some green space. This space would disappear and ensure that the local residents would have to travel to a park over a mile away to walk their dogs or play with their children.
Candidate B: Hi I don't like the plans for the flats as it means that we won't be able to go to the park anymore. It also means that there will be more people using public transport. The public transport in the area is awful so you need to improve that as well as it really annoys me when it gets delayed.
Candidate C: Dear Sir or Madam Please don't build the flats on my local park. I feel very strongly about this as I really like the park and it will affect my quality of life if you do this. I have lived here all my life and it will ruin the place where I live.

3. Copy the table below and tick the features each example answer has. Then note down two or three strengths and weakness of each answer.

	A	B	C
The salutation is appropriate to the audience.			
The tone is formal.			
There is a wide range of vocabulary.			
The letter is relevant to the task (about building on a park).			
The letter has personal opinion.			
The opening paragraph presents a clear point of argument.			
The letter contains a range of sentence types.			

Speeches

You may be asked to write a script for a speech in the exam. Make sure you:

- demonstrate awareness of who your audience is
- show that you understand the purpose of your speech
- use a clear structure
- use appropriate language and tone.

Openings

- Make an impact and show the audience that you know who they are.
- Make sure you establish your text as a speech by beginning for example, *Ladies and gentlemen, I am delighted to be here this afternoon…*

> **Examiner tip**
>
> The opening is where you can show the examiner the audience of your speech. For example, if you start with 'Ladies and Gentleman', the examiner can tell that you are aiming your speech at adults.

Body of the speech

- Use paragraphs, each one with a specific focus that links to the task.
- Use a range of appropriate rhetorical devices for effect.

Endings

Try to end decisively or with a call to action for the audience. You want them to remember what you have said and the ending must stay with them.

Activity 7

1. Look at the extract from a speech on the next page, written in response to the exam-style question. Use a printout to circle or underline the rhetorical devices the writer has used.

> Write the text for a speech outlining the benefits of becoming a vegetarian.

> Ladies and Gentlemen.
>
> I want to talk to you today about the need for us all to become vegetarian. I know what you are thinking: 'Here we go – another 16 year old who is worried about the plight of cows and chickens and how they shouldn't be killed for their meat'. Well, that is one of the reasons why we should all become vegetarian, but there are so many more reasons why we all should consider this. It is vital for the environment, it is vital for the economy and it is vital for everyone's health.
>
> Let me start with the environmental improvements we could bring about if we all became vegetarian for just two days a week. We could all commit to that, surely? By doing this, we could reduce our greenhouse gas emissions by 10% and this would rise to 33% if we could all commit to a meat- and fish-free diet for life. Wow!
>
> Now, I know how difficult this would be. We all like a bacon sandwich for our breakfast and a juicy steak for our dinner, but if the production of these treats is having such a negative impact on our environment, don't we owe it to ourselves and future generations to consider an alternative food source?

2. Copy the table below, giving specific examples from the text and explaining the effect they have on the reader. One example has been completed for you.

Rhetorical device	Example	Effect on the reader
Rhetorical questions	We can all commit to that, surely?	Makes the reader feel the writer is talking to them.
Facts and statistics		
Personal pronouns		
Sentence lengths		
Emotive language		
Imperative sentences		
Personal anecdotes		
Flattery		
Triplets		

Checking your work

Punctuation: Make sure you have included appropriate and accurate punctuation.

Word choice and spelling: Check you have used a wide range of vocabulary to engage your reader and have not used the same word repeatedly.

Paragraphing: Make sure you have used separate paragraphs for each new point that you make to guide your reader through your ideas in a logical way.

Grammar and style: Make sure you have not changed tense by mistake. Check you have maintained the same tone and register throughout your piece.

Sentences: Check you have used a variety of sentence structures.

> **Examiner tip**
>
> You can use the // symbol in your work if you have missed out a paragraph break in your exam response.

Assessment test

Exam guidance

> **Texts**
>
> This Assessment test section is based on three texts: *The Haunted Hotel* by Wilkie Collins, *My Family and Other Animals* by Gerald Durrell and 'Are you struggling with expat culture shock?' by Joseph Shaules.

Paper 1

Read the text below and answer Questions 1–4 on the question paper.

The Haunted Hotel: **by Wilkie Collins**

In this extract, Agnes is staying in a hotel in Venice. She is staying in the same hotel where Montbarry, her dead ex-fiancé and his new wife, the Countess, once stayed.

How long that first sleep lasted, she never knew. She could only remember, in the after-time, that she woke instantly.

Every faculty and perception in her passed the boundary line between insensibility* and consciousness, so to speak, at a leap. Without knowing why, she sat up suddenly in the bed, listening for she knew not what. Her head was in a whirl; her heart beat furiously, without any assignable cause. But one trivial event had happened during the interval while she had been asleep. The night-light had gone out; and the room, as a matter of course, was in total darkness. 5

She felt for the match-box, and paused after finding it. A vague sense of confusion was still in her mind. She was in no hurry to light the match. The pause in the darkness was, for the moment, agreeable to her. 10

In the quieter flow of her thoughts during this interval, she could ask herself the natural question: – What cause had awakened her so suddenly, and had so strangely shaken her nerves? Had it been the influence of a dream? She had not dreamed at all – or to speak more correctly, she had no waking remembrance of having dreamed. The mystery was beyond her fathoming**: the darkness began to oppress*** her. She struck the match on the box, and lit her candle. 15

As the welcome light diffused itself over the room, she turned from the table and looked towards the other side of the bed.

In the moment when she turned, the chill of a sudden terror gripped her round her heart, as with the clasp of an icy hand.

She was not alone in the room! 20

There – in the chair at her bedside – there, suddenly revealed under the flow of light from the candle, was the figure of a woman, reclining. Her head lay back over the chair. Her face, turned up to the ceiling, had the eyes closed, as if she was wrapped in a deep sleep.

The shock of the discovery held Agnes speechless and helpless. Her first conscious action, when she was in some degree mistress of herself again, was to lean over the bed and to look closer at the woman who had 25 so incomprehensibly stolen into her room in the dead of night. One glance was enough: she started back with a cry of amazement. The person in the chair was no other than the widow of the dead Montbarry – the woman who had warned her that they were to meet again, and that the place might be Venice!

Her courage returned to her, stung in action by the natural sense of indignation, which the presence of the Countess provoked. 30

'Wake up!' she called out. 'How dare you come here? How did you get in? Leave the room – or I will call for help!'

She raised her voice at the last words. It produced no effect. Leaning further over the bed, she boldly took the Countess by the shoulder and shook her. Not even this effect succeeded in rousing the sleeping woman. She still lay back in the chair, possessed by a torpor**** like the torpor of death – 35 insensible to sound, insensible to touch. Was she really sleeping? Or had she fainted?

Agnes looked closer at her. She had not fainted. Her breathing was audible in gasps. At intervals she ground her teeth savagely. Beads of perspiration stood thickly on her forehead. Her clenched hands rose and fell slowly from time to time on her lap. Was she in the agony of a dream? Or was she spiritually conscious of something hidden in the room? 40

The doubt involved in that last question was unendurable. Agnes determined to rouse the servants who kept watch in the hotel at night.

*insensibility** – lack of awareness
*fathoming*** – understanding
*oppress**** – to lie heavily upon; to weigh down
*torpor***** – lack of movement; coma-like state

Assessment Test

Paper 1

Section A – Reading

Read the text in the Reading Text insert provided and answer ALL questions.

You should spend about 1 hour on this section.

Write your answers on a separate sheet of paper.

1   From lines 3–5, identify the phrase which describes how Agnes reacted when she woke up.

(Total for Question 1 = 1 mark)

2   From lines 6–12, give **two** ways in which the writer shows Agnes' changing state of mind. You may use your own words or quotations from the text.

(Total for Question 2 = 2 marks)

3   In lines 13–24, how does the writer use language and structure to show Agnes' gradual understanding of her situation? Support your views with reference to the text.

(Total for Question 3 = 6 marks)

4   In this extract, there is an attempt to create suspense. Evaluate how successfully this is achieved. Support your views with detailed reference to the text.

(Total for Question 4 = 15 marks)

Assessment Test

Section B: Imaginative Writing

Answer ONE question. You should spend about 45 minutes on this section.

Write your answers on a separate sheet of paper.

EITHER

1 *Look at the images provided.

Write about a dream you have or have had.

Your response could be real or imagined.

You may wish to base your response on one of the images.

Your response will be marked for the accurate and appropriate use of vocabulary, spelling, punctuation and grammar.

OR

2 *Write about a time when you or someone you know had a surprising experience.

Your response could be real or imagined.

You may wish to base your response on one of the images.

Your response will be marked for the accurate and appropriate use of vocabulary, spelling, punctuation and grammar.

Images

Paper 2

Read the text below and answer Questions 1–3 on the question paper.

Text 1

***My Family and Other Animals*: by Gerald Durrell**

In this extract taken from My Family and Other Animals, *Gerald Durrell explains how both he and his family (including his dog, Roger), settled into their new life in the Greek Island of Corfu after moving there from England in 1935.*

I came to know the plump peasant girls who passed the garden every morning and evening. Riding side-saddle on their slouching, drooping-eared donkeys, they were shrill and colourful as parrots, and their characters and laughter echoed among the olive trees. In the mornings they would smile and shout greetings as their donkeys pattered past, and in the evenings they would lean over the fuchsia hedge, balancing precariously on their steeds' back, and smiling, hold out gifts for me – a bunch of amber grapes, still sun-warmed, some figs, black as tar, striped with pink where they had burst their seams with ripeness, or a giant watermelon with an inside like pink ice. As the days passed I came gradually to understand them. What had at first been a confused babble became a series of recognisable separate sounds. Then, suddenly, these took on meaning and slowly and haltingly I started to use them myself; then I took my newly acquired words and strung them into ungrammatical and stumbling sentences. Our neighbours were delighted, as though I had conferred* some delicate compliment by trying to learn their language. They would lean over the hedge, their faces screwed up with concentration, as I groped my way through a greeting or a simple remark, and when I had successfully concluded they would beam at me, nodding and smiling, and clap their hands. By degrees, I learned their names, who was related to whom, which were married and which hoped to be, and other details. I learned where their little cottages were among the olive groves, and should Roger and I chance to pass that way, the entire family, vociferous** and pleased, would tumble out to greet us, to bring a chair, so that I might sit under their vine and eat some fruit with them.

Gradually the magic of the island settled over us as gently and clingingly as pollen. Each day had a tranquillity, a timelessness about it, so that you wished it would never end. But then the dark skin of night would peel off and there would be a fresh day waiting for us, glossy and colourful as a child's transfer*** and with the same tinge of unreality.

*conferred** – granted/given
*vociferous*** – loud and forceful
*child's transfer**** – popular in the 1970s, an image printed on clear paper which could be scribbled over to transfer onto a piece of paper

Read the text below and answer Questions 4–6 on the question paper.

Text 2

'Are you struggling with expat culture shock?': by Joseph Shaules

In this article from The Daily Telegraph, the author and educator, Joseph Shaules, discusses the struggles expatriates, or expats, face when they move abroad.

Why is it that intelligent, emotionally healthy people sometimes struggle to adjust to life abroad? Cathy was a vivacious Asian-American who was excited about moving to Tokyo and confident she would adapt easily. Yet Cathy was blindsided*: 'I became negative and withdrawn – the complete opposite of the person I really am.'

Hasn't today's global society taken us beyond culture shock? As an educator who has worked with expatriates for years, the answer is clear – No. Even educated, cosmopolitan expats can be affected.

As I discuss in my book, *The Intercultural Mind*, recent advances in psychology are helping us understand why. The root of the issue lies in the unconscious – the 'auto pilot' that guides you through the routines of everyday life. Your unconscious mind is highly sensitive to new patterns abroad.

There are three common reactions to going abroad: culture surprise, culture stress and culture shock.

Culture surprise refers to the wonder that comes when you notice differences in foreign places. Your unconscious is alerting your conscious mind to anomalies**. Cathy noticed signs in Japanese, rice fields, plastic food in restaurant display cases. Even aspects of life abroad you think you are prepared for can be surprising. When Kentaro moved from Japan to Canada he knew it was an English-speaking country, but was unprepared for what that would feel like. Even minor differences – the portion sizes, the lack of trains – can feel quite alien.

This novelty can be exciting, but it also creates mental strain experienced as culture stress. Your mental batteries get depleted*** from focusing your attention and solving problems. More than exotic customs, it's the difficulty of accomplishing everyday tasks – looking for shampoo or using a foreign ATM – that tires your mind. When Jane moved to Shanghai, she said that the bustle of the city had been exciting at first, but combined with a hunt for a simple loaf of wholemeal bread it soon made her irritable and judgmental.

Because these processes are unconscious, it is difficult to prepare. Cathy spent many hours researching her new home in Tokyo – even using Google Maps to learn the streets around her flat. 'I felt like I was an expert,' she says, 'but how wrong I was! Nothing had prepared me for having to try and function "normally".'

You may not notice that the strain is building until you feel culture shock – a potentially powerful yet vague sense of malaise**** or depression. It results from the processes in your unconscious mind being overwhelmed by new patterns. Unlike culture stress, which arises out of particular situations, culture shock may seem to come out of nowhere.

Fortunately, your mental processes have lots of built-in flexibility. As you establish new routines, you get your mental autopilot back on track. Cathy found that she felt increasingly at home abroad. 'When it was time to go back home,' she reports, 'I was in tears at having to leave.' Until then, remember to take your time adjusting (forcing yourself to keep exploring can sometimes backfire), reach out to others if you are struggling and be mindful of the way you are feeling.

Assessment Test

Culture shock remains with us in the 21st century because its root causes are built into the architecture of our minds. Living abroad is not simply a long holiday – it taxes mental resources. Yet it is often also a source of growth. The strains of adjustment, far from indicating a problem, are part of what makes your stay meaningful. Moving abroad is what you make of the challenges it presents.

*blindsided** – to be knocked off balance or taken by surprise
*anomalies*** – things that are different
*depleted**** – used up/worn out
*malaise***** – feeling of unhappiness

Assessment Test

Section A – Reading

You should spend about 1 hour and 15 minutes on the WHOLE of section A (Questions 1–7).

Read Text 1. Then answer Questions 1–3.

Write your answers on a separate sheet of paper.

1   From lines 1–7, identify **two** things the peasant girls did as they passed by the garden.

(Total for Question 1 = 2 marks)

2   From lines 14–17, give **two** pieces of information the writer learns about his neighbours. You may use your own words or quotations from the text.

(Total for Question 2 = 2 marks)

3   Analyse how the writer uses language and structure to engage the reader.

In your answer you should write about:

- language features and techniques
- structural features and techniques
- the effect on the reader.

Support your views with detailed reference to the text.

(Total for Question 3 = 15 marks)

Read Text 2. Then answer Questions 4–6.

Write your answers on a separate sheet of paper.

4   From lines 33–35, identify **one** piece of advice the writer offers to anyone who might be struggling to adjust to life in a new country.

(Total for Question 4 = 1 mark)

5   In lines 30–32, identify the phrase which shows how Jane felt after she had been in Shanghai for a while.

(Total for Question 5 = 1 mark)

6   In this extract, the writer attempts to engage the reader by explaining what to expect when you move to a new country.

Evaluate how successfully this is achieved.

Support your views with detailed references to the text.

(Total for Question 6 = 15 marks)

Question 7 is about Text 1 and Text 2.

Answer BOTH parts of the question. Refer to BOTH texts in your answers.

Write your answers on a separate sheet of paper.

7 a The two texts show the experience of people moving to a new country.

What similarities do the people share in these extracts?

Use evidence from both texts to support your answer.

b Compare how the writers of Text 1 and Text 2 present ideas and perspectives about living abroad.

You should write about:

- the ideas and perspectives of the writers
- how they are presented
- how they are similar/different.

Support your answer with detailed references to the texts.

Section B: Transactional Writing

Answer ONE question. You should spend about 45 minutes on this section.

Write your answers on a separate sheet of paper.

EITHER

8 *Write a text for a speech you will give to your peers about whether it is important to learn to speak another language.

In your speech you could include:

- how another language might help you when you travel abroad
- whether it would have any impact on job opportunities in the future
- what the obstacles are to learning another language

as well as any other ideas you might have.

Your response will be marked for the accurate and appropriate use of vocabulary, spelling, punctuation and grammar.

OR

9 *You have seen a brochure from a college in another country which offers a range of academic and vocational courses.

Write a letter of application to the head of the college outlining why you would like to study there.

In your application, you could:

- outline why you would be a good student for the college
- consider what problems you might need to overcome
- suggest how you would overcome these problems

as well as any other ideas you might have.

Your response will be marked for the accurate and appropriate use of vocabulary, spelling, punctuation and grammar.

English terms

Alliteration	When two or more words positioned close to each other begin with the same sound (for example, 'The grass grew green.')
Anecdotes	Real life stories or examples
Atmosphere	The feelings that a text creates for the reader, conveyed through language choice
Autobiography	Writing about yourself, usually your life story; a period of time in your life or a specific experience you have had
Broadsheet newspaper	A newspaper that focuses more on serious news stories with a greater focus on good reporting and writing
Chronological order	In time order from beginning to end
Clause	A group of words, often smaller than a full sentence, containing a verb
Compare	Identify similarities and differences
Conjunction	A word used to connect clauses or sentences (e.g. 'and', 'if', 'but')
Connotation	An idea, feeling or impression that a word or phrase creates in the reader's mind
Contrast	Using two opposite ideas
Deduction	Drawing a conclusion based on general principles or evidence
Direct speech	The exact words spoken by a person, using speech marks and followed by a reporting verb such as 'said', or 'cried'
Emotive	Something that is likely to cause an emotional response, for example, shock, upset
Emotive language	Powerful word choices which influence the reader's emotional response
Emphasis	Stress given to a word when speaking
Explicit	Expressed directly and with no possibility of confusion
Foreshadow	Predict
Formal language	A less personal style of language – more commonly used when writing
Ideas	Points the writer makes about the topic
Impact	The effect that the writer wants the text to have on the reader
Implicit	Suggested rather than expressed directly
Inference	An idea or piece of information that a writer suggests, but does not state clearly or explicitly. It can be referred to as 'reading between the lines'.
Informal language	A more personal style of language – more commonly used when speaking
Intention	The impact and effect that the writer wants the text to have on the reader
Interpret	Read between the lines to come to a conclusion
Intonation	The rise and fall of the voice when speaking
Metaphor	A direct comparison made without using 'like' or 'as' (for example, 'My father was a charging rhinoceros.')
Mood	The atmosphere or feelings that a text creates for the reader, conveyed through language choice
Narrative prose	The telling of a story, written in continuous prose rather than poetry
Narrator	The person who tells the story
Onomatopoeia	A word that sounds like the sound it represents (for example, 'crash', 'bang', 'whoosh', etc.)
Parallel	Using two similar ideas
Personification	Describing something that is not human using language associated with humans (for example, 'The grass whispered and the leaves danced in the breeze.')
Perspectives	The writer's views about the topic
Phrase	A sequence of two or more words arranged in a grammatical construction and acting as a unit in a sentence
Protagonist	The main character in a novel
Purpose	The overall aim of a text
Quotation	A group of words taken from a text and copied exactly as they appeared in the text
Register	The language used to create a style of writing, or used by a certain group of people (formal or informal)
Reported speech	A report of what someone said, not using their exact words
Rhetorical device	A technique used in writing or speaking to influence or persuade the audience
Sentence	A set of words that is complete in itself. It can be identified as beginning with a capital letter and ending with a final punctuation mark such as a full stop, question mark, or exclamation mark.
Simile	A comparison made using 'like' or 'as' (for example, 'My father ran like a charging rhinoceros.')
Strapline	A heading used in adverts. It is usually larger than the rest of the text, in a prominent position, and written to grab the reader's attention and make them read on
Structural shift	A turning point or change in a text, for example in mood, viewpoint or argument in a written text
Synthesis	Bringing together related elements, information or ideas in two or more texts
Tabloid newspaper	A newspaper that reports current events but also focuses on popular stories, for example, about celebrities
Tone	The way a writer expresses a certain attitude or mood through their language choices. This can often help the reader imagine the voice of the narrator or writer.
Topic sentence	Usually the first sentence in a paragraph which signposts the topic of the text that follows
Verb	A word used to describe an action, state or occurrence
Word class	A category of word that defines the function the word has in a sentence. Categories include noun, verb, adjective, adverb, pronoun, etc.
Written in the first person	The writer uses the pronoun 'I'.
Written in the third person	The writer uses pronouns such as 'she', 'it', 'they', etc. to refer to people in the text.